Remains of Arabic in the Spanish and Portuguese languages. With a sketch by way of introduction of the history of Spain, : from the invasion to the expulsion of the Moors. Also extracts from the original letters in Arabic to and from Don Manoueel and his

Stephen Weston

Nabu Public Domain Reprints:

You are holding a reproduction of an original work published before 1923 that is in the public domain in the United States of America, and possibly other countries. You may freely copy and distribute this work as no entity (individual or corporate) has a copyright on the body of the work. This book may contain prior copyright references, and library stamps (as most of these works were scanned from library copies). These have been scanned and retained as part of the historical artifact.

This book may have occasional imperfections such as missing or blurred pages, poor pictures, errant marks, etc. that were either part of the original artifact, or were introduced by the scanning process. We believe this work is culturally important, and despite the imperfections, have elected to bring it back into print as part of our continuing commitment to the preservation of printed works worldwide. We appreciate your understanding of the imperfections in the preservation process, and hope you enjoy this valuable book.

REMAINS OF ARABIC

IN THE

SPANISH AND PORTUGUESE LANGUAGES.

WITH A

SKETCH BY WAY OF INTRODUCTION

OF THE

HISTORY OF SPAIN,

FROM THE

INVASION TO THE EXPULSION OF THE MOORS.

ALSO

EXTRACTS FROM THE ORIGINAL LETTERS IN ARABIC
TO AND FROM DON MANOUEEL AND HIS
GOVERNORS IN INDIA AND AFRICA.

APPENDIX,

CONTAINING A

SPECIMEN OF THE INTRODUCTION TO THE
HITOPADESA TRANSLATED INTO THREE LANGUAGES,
THE PRINCIPAL METRE OF WHICH IS THAT OF
THE SANSCRIT.

Y este nombre Albogues es Morisco, como lo son todos aquellos, que en nostra lengua Castellana comienςan en AL. D. Quixote, Part. iv. Lib. viii. Cap. lxvii.

By *STEPHEN WESTON*, B.D. F.R.S. S.A.

PRINTED BY S. ROUSSEAU, WOOD STREET, SPA FIELDS;

AND SOLD BY

PAYNE, PALL MALL; AND CLARK, NEW BOND STREET.

1810.

LOAN STACK

ADVERTISEMENT.

THE introduction to this small work is intended to give a slight outline of the history of the Moors, from their invasion of Spain in the beginning of the eighth century, to their expulsion from it in the end of the fifteenth.

The passage in the title from Cervantes arose from a question of Sancho, concerning the word Albogues, which he had never before heard, or seen in all his life. Upon which Don Quixote tells him that it is an Arabic word, as all the words are in Spanish which begin with Al, and that there are only three Arabic words in Spanish which end in I, and that they are, Borçegui, Zaquiçami, and Maravedi, since Aheli, and Alfaqui are known to be Arabic by their prefix. We learn from Athenæus, p. 66. F. that there is but one Greek word ending in I, and that is μέλι, honey, since πέπερι, κόμμι, κοῖφι, pepper, gum, and koiphy, a confection used for an antidote, are foreigners. Albogue for the most part means a pipe, or flute, made of reeds joined together; hard to blow, and of a grating sound, when ill-played; like the shepherd's in Virgil, Eclog. iii. 27.

— — "non tu in triviis indocte solebas
Stridenti miserum stipula disperdere carmen;"

which Milton has admirably expressed in a word of his own,

"When they list, their lean and flashy songs,
Grate on their scrannel pipes of wretched straw."

In Don Quixote however, Albogues is explained to be brass plates like flat candlesticks, which, beat together, make a rustic music, such as provoked Hotspur to say,

"I had rather hear a brazen can'stick turn'd,
Or a dry wheel grate on the axle-tree."
Henry IV. Part i. Act iii. Scene i.

INTRODUCTION.

INTRODUCTION.

THE Goths, who had driven the Romans out of Spain, were, in their turn, put to flight by the Saracens, whom Count Julien had called in to revenge himself on Roderic, the dishonourer of his daughter. The Christians of Spain having submitted to the Moors, were called Muzarabes, that is, Meseehee-Arabes, or Arabs of Messiah, because they retained their own religious worship. Roderic was the last Gothic king in Spain, in 714, and Pelage, his near relation, hid himself in the rocks of Asturia, and after three years concealment sallied forth from his sanctuary, Notre Dame de Covagonda, a grot amidst inaccessible rocks; when full of hope and ardent zeal, and followed by numerous partisans, he drove back the usurpers, who, unable to cut him off, entered into negociation, and suffered him to enjoy a certain district, provided he paid them a small tribute in acknowledgement of their superiority as chief Lords paramount of the Seigniory. In process of time he was again insulted by the Moors, whom he marched against, and defeated in the year 716, and recovered whole provinces, and was proclaimed King of Leon and the Asturias, and reigned till 737, twenty years, with an exemplary reputation for true piety and determined courage; without libertinum, and without luxury. This part of his character may possibly have been the reason, why Voltaire has refused to call him a king. It is, however, to him that the Christian kings of Spain, owe the preservation of the title of sovereign; who, in after-times, once more expelled the Moors under Philip the Third. The strength of the Christians was mightily augmented by the intestine divisions of the Moors. In 745, Don Alonzo, the Catholic son-in-law to Pelagio, passed the mountains, and came upon the northern part of Galicia, and in a single campaign, unopposed by any great or commanding force, conquered nearly the whole of that province.

Next

Next year he attacked Leon and Castille, and reduced Astorga, Leon, and Saldagna, before the Moors could bring an equal force to cope with him, and possessed himself of Montes de Oca, Amaya, and Alava, at the foot of the mountains. The year after he pushed on towards Portugal, and ravaged the country as far as Castille; but not being able to protect his conquests in the flats, which he had subdued, he burnt and laid waste the plains, led the Christians back to the mountains, and carried off the Moors for slaves. Thus encompassed by a desert of his own making he remained quiet for some years, and as he grew stronger he occupied the champaign country by degrees, and rebuilt the cities he had demolished of Leon and Astorgas. He died in 757, and was succeeded by his son, Don Froila, who had partaken of his conquests, and fought by his side. During his reign the Saracens in Spain threw off the yoke of the Khalif, and Abderrahman, the viceroy, rendered himself independent, and fixed the seat of his government at Cordova. The consequence was, that the divisions of the Moors were settled, but for all this Froila took their general prisoner, and killed and routed 54,000 of them in a pitched battle, and then built Oviedo, and made it his capital for the convenience of defending the level plains which he had begun to people. Abderrahman called also Abderame, was captain general, and governor of Spain, for Hescham Khalif, of the race of the Ommiads, in the year 113 of the Hejira, and 731 of our reckoning. It was he that Charles Martel defeated near Poitiers in 732, when the battle lasted a whole day, and the slaughter of the Saracens was immense.

There are Arabic coins in some cabinets struck under the first Emirs of Spain, and afterwards by Musa son of Nasir, or rather by Alahor son of Abderrahman Alsasak, (who came from Hispalis, and settled at Corduba,) from the year 100. Chr. 718, A. D. to Abderrahman the Third, in the year 300, or 912 of Christ.

Abderrahman son of Moavie, and grandson

son of Hefcham Khalif, of the Ommiads, came to Spain when he was twenty-eight years old, in the 756th year of Jefus Chrift, when Almanfor was Khalif of Bagdat. This fugitive prince was recognifed, and acknowledged by the Arabs in the Weft to be the legitimate Khalif, and reigned thirty-two years, and fome months, and left his crown to his fon Hefcham, in the year 172 of the Hejira. It was he that built the great Mofque of Cordova in 170, and founded the monarchy which lafted till 335 or 946 of our Era. He was called El Adel, the Juft: he left eleven fons and nine daughters, according to Khondemir Ebn-Amid, but the years and the dates differ in the Spanifh Chronicle. Abderrahman fecond of the name was the fon of Hakem, and grandfon of Hefcham, and the fourth Khalif of Spain, of the race of the Ommiads; he reigned thirty-one years, and died in 852, leaving forty-five fons, and forty-two daughters. Under his government the Mohammedans fplit into various factions, and waged war with one another. During thefe diforders the

Chriftians

Christians retook Barcelona; but on order being restored, Abderrahman conquered it again, and with it the city of Valencia, which his uncle had persuaded to revolt against him; he there chased, and dispersed a fleet of Norman ships that came from Lisbon for the purpose of taking possession of Cadix and Seville; and having silenced his foreign enemies, and appeased his domestic broils, turned himself to the arts of peace, and paved the city of Cordova, and brought water to it by a noble and costly aqueduct. There was also a third Abderrahman, the eighth Khalif of the same family, that reigned nearly sixty years in Spain. Ebn Amid tells us, that he was the son of Almondir, and was surnamed after having been proclaimed Khalif, Nasser-ledin-illah. He succeeded his brother Abdallah in the 300th year of the Hegira. It was this prince who first took the title of the Commander of the Faithful, Emir Almoumenin during the divisions for the succession to the Khaliphate, in which violent efforts were made on the side of the Abbassides on one

part,

part, and the Ommiads of the other: Nevertheless Abderrahman kept possession of the government through the whole extent of the West for a space of fifty years, and died quietly at the age of seventy-four in the year 350, that is, 961 of our account.

There is in Wise's Catalogue of the Bodleian Coins, one, which Gagnier says, was struck at Alexandria, Anno 310, Chr. 912, that really belongs to the reign of Abderrahman III. and the mint of Andalusia. The coins of the early Khalifs, that resided at Corduba, have on them Andalus, which was the name given by the Moors to Spain, and the word Corduba is to be supplied, as Panormus is in the Sicilian coins, which read only Medeenet Sikileet.

In the year 979, when the Christians were on the point of a total subjugation of the Moors, and little short of being rid of them for ever, appeared Mohammed Ebn Emir Almanzor, a Saracen General, who by a series of bold and successful enterprises turned the scale, and inspired his countrymen with new

courage

courage to maintain their post, and recover their lost ground. Almanzor was the grand Vizeer to the King of Cordova, and, irritated against the Christians, from the sufferings of the Moors, became furious and implacable in his warfare. He took Leon, and putting the inhabitants to the sword, burnt the town. Barcelona met with a similar treatment, and Castille was ravaged; Galicia and Portugal overrun and plundered. The Christians were every where beat, and never won a battle in the course of forty different actions, in which they fought the Saracens; but as small obstacles sometimes turn great torrents out of their course, so on the taking of Compostella, and at the carrying off in triumph of the gates of the church of St. James, a flux broke out among the troops of the infidels, which the Christians naturally interpreting a stroke from Heaven, for sacrilege committed against the church of their favourite saint, attacked the conquerors in their turn with such a holy rage, and divine fury, that not all the cool courage of Almanzor could rally the fugitives

of

of his terror-struck troops; when totally unable to make any stand he was himself reduced to run away, and, leaving his followers to their fate, he fled to Medina Celi, and died of regret and abstinence in the year 998. We have a coin extant that was struck under the Khalif Hescham Almuaeed Billah, who reigned from 976 to 1008. See Tychsen, p. 132. Tab. lxiii. It is of silver, and has on it in the area, There is no God but God, and none like him. Round the margin, In the name of God, this Dirhem was struck in Andalus, in the year seventy and three hundred. On the reverse, Iman Hescham, prince of the faithful Almuaeed Billah, Aamer, that is, Royal.

During these times, the kingdom of Castille arose, and as yet undivided. Old Castille was set up long before the New had been recovered from the Moor, and separated from Leon by some insignificant streams on one side, and bounded by Asturias, Biscay, and Rioja on the other, a province belonging

formerly

formerly to Navarre, now annexed to Old Castille, whose principal towns are Logrono, Calzada, Najara, and Bellorado. This district soon became a bone of contention between the sovereigns of Leon and Cordova, and as the former were more fortunate in war than the latter, the nobles of Castille became independent in spite of the Moors, when their power was in its meridian. The kings also of Leon, and Oviedo, and Castille, united in the year 1035. when Don Sanchez bestowed Castille, which had fallen under his power, on his eldest son Don Ferdinand with the title of King; and thus the sovereigns became kings of Leon and Castille, by the union of the territories of Castille with those of Leon and Oviedo. And now another kingdom arose, the kingdom of Arragon, and about the year 1035, Don Sanchez, surnamed the Great, king of Navarre, raised Arragon into a government for his son Don Ramira. At this time the whole of Spain was divided into two unequal parts, by a boundary drawn from East to West, from Valentia to a point somewhat be-

low

low the mouth of the Douro. All to the North of this line was Christian, the smallest and the poorest portion of the country, and all to the South Moorish, and by far the richest share in all senses. There was nothing wanting in the Moors but union to be masters of the whole, and so it may be said of the other party, for feuds and divisions prevailed within and without in both camps,

> Seditione, dolis, scelere, atque libidine, et ira
> Hesperios intra muros peccatur, et extra.

Although the Christians did not draw up in battle-array as the Moors were in the habit of doing, one against another, yet they too quarrelled bitterly and implacably, and were always ready to call in foreign aid to terminate a domestic broil, which was an incalculable advantage to their enemies, sua si bona norint, had they known how to take it. The divisions, however, of the Moors were more minute; and every town had its sovereign, who was jealous of some neighbour, so that they both, one after another, fell a prey to an invader, since each preferred to be ru-

ined

ined and cut up singly, rather than by uniting risk the chance of the aggrandizement of a sister city, at the expence of any aid and assistance against the common enemy. The consequence was easily foreseen. The king of Toledo is at war with his brother of Seville, Alphonso stands by, and, watching the lucky moment of attack, pounces upon Toledo and all its dependencies, and makes it his capital, soon after the province of New Castille is reduced; and Madrid, a petty town, becomes the property of the Christians. So much did Alphonso, King of Castille, for want of common confidence of one Moorish kingdom in another, from the year 1080 to 1084.

The city of Toledo had been a long time in the hands of the Goths, but was conquered in the year 715 by the Mohammedans, and changed its master. To the year 764 it underwent a variety of vicissitude and internal disturbance, and was stormed by Nader and Taman, generals of the Spanish Khalif Abderrahman. Deguignes, p. 61. T. i. In 828 it revolted with many other cities under a

leader

leader of the name of Haſſan, and was not brought back to the obedience of the Khalif, till nine years afterwards. At the extinction of the Ommiad ſovereigns, Toledo renounced her Mohammedan kings Beni Dulnum, that had governed her from 435 to 478, or from 1043 to 1085. Then came Alphons, the ſon of Sancho, King of Caſtille, and drove them out, and took their city from them; and from that period, except a ſhort interval, it remained in the poſſeſſion of the Chriſtians, from the year 1195 to 1212. See Deguignes Hiſtoire des Huns, tom. i. par. i. pp. 321, 51, 56, 58. Alphons the VIIIth, ſon of Sancho III. whoſe coins are dated at Caſtille and Toledo, ſucceeded his father 1158, and having reigned fifty-five years, died in 1214. As it happens that the conquered adopt the laws preſcribed by the conqueror, ſo the Arabians brought with them into Spain their language and their literature; and the Spaniards applied themſelves with ſo much zeal and ardour that they became acquainted intimately with the elegance of the Arabic tongue, and wrote poems which the Moors admired, to the utter neglect of their vernacular language, so that, not one Spaniard in a thousand could compose a plain letter of compliment, or transact business in Spanish, or Latin, when whole colleges excelled in writing Arabic, with all the pride of learning, and the pomp of calligraphy. The proof of this is to be sought for in Alvarus de Corduba whose Manuscript of the Church of Cordova P. Florez published in España Sagra, tom. i. p. 274, ita ut in omni Christ. Collegio vix inveniatur unus in milleno hominum numero qui salutorius fratri possit rationaliter dirigere literas, et reperiantur absque numero multiplices turbæ, quæ erudite Arabicas verborum explicent pompas. The women also cultivated the muses of Mecca, and Maria Alfaisuli of Seville, obtained the title of the Arabian Sappho. Her works are in the Escurial. She flourished in 411, which is equal to 1020 of our reckoning. See Casiri, tom. i. p. 150. Arab. Hispan. Escurialensis. It is therefore no great matter of surprise, that Alfons, a Christian prince,

should

should have struck his coins with Arabic legends, since his subjects were more familiar with that than any other language, not excepting their own, but the astonishment is, that he should not have had the fear of the Moors before his eyes, and the dread of affronting the Mohammedans, his near and irreconcileable enemies, by the insulting use of their language, which they must, no doubt, look upon as polluted, and contaminated in the service of the Cross. The Moors, however, were not intolerant, and permitted the full exercise of the Christian religion in the towns which were subject to them. Ambrosio de Morales, l. c. fol. 207. tells us, Los Moros dexaron a los Christianos con sus dignidades sacerdotes, y grande uso en su religion. We may then, to say the least, pronounce the Castillian monarch guilty of an indiscretion; though we admire his spirit and intrepidity. The gold Cufic coins of Toledo were in the Borgian collection, and have been published by Adler at Rome, in the year 1782, they are nearly all alike, that is, the inscription is

C the

the same on all, but the date different. They are four in number. In the area is a cross, the word Ulmesecheea, or Christian, and under it ALF. Alfons. Round the margin, In the name of the Father, the Son, and Holy Ghost, the only God. On the reverse. In the area, Emeer of the Franks, Catholicks, Alfons ben Sancho, by the hand, power, and grace of God. Round the margin, This coin was struck in the city of Talitala, in the year 1185. The next in the year 1186, the third 1191, the fourth 1182. Toletam, or Toledo, in Arabic is Talitala according to Abulfaragius, in his History of the Dynasties, p. 241. See Pocock. Alfons in his challenge, 1194, to James, or Jacob, king of Africa, shewed a temper of mind for courage not easily daunted. Abulfarage has preserved this letter, p. 412. lat. vers. p. 277. But to resume the thread of my history; the Moors were so much alarmed at the loss of Toledo and Madrid, that they collected a great force, and with the additional succour of Mohammed Ben Joseph, king of Barbary, who came at their call with

his

his myriads, and fought the Christians and defeated them on the 16th of July, on the borders of Andalusia, in the Sierra Morena, or Black Mountains, so called because its ridges rise, and fall like a saw. It is a provincial saying in Spain, When it snows here, what does it on the Saw? Quando aqui nieva, que harà en la Sierra? This victory is celebrated annually at Toledo, but as if satisfied with the greatness of the effort they had made, the Christians dispersed, and the Moors strengthened by the remains of the men from Barbary united again to try their fortune, but for want of confidence they fell out among themselves, and having no central force, every attempt ended in defeat, and loss of territory. In 1236, Don Ferdinand, of Castille and Leon, took the city of Cordova, the residence of the first Moorish kings, with Murcia, Seville, Xeres, Cadix, and St. Lucar, whilst James, or Jayine I. of Aragon, seized Majorca, Minorca, and Valentia, and drove the Moors before him. Ferdinand III. son of Alphonse IX. was cousin-german of St.

Louis, and entertained the project of subduing the kingdom of Morocco, as Louis did of conquering Palæstine. In 1308, Ferdinand IV. king of Castille, made war on the king of Granada, and took the fortress of Gibraltar. He was a violent prince, passionate to excess, and despotic; he acquired the name of El Prorogado, or the adjourned, because in a fit of rage he ordered two of his nobles to be thrown over a Tarpeian Rock, or precipice, and they, before the execution of the sentence, cited him to appear before God in thirty hours, to give an account of this act of tyranny; and at the end of this period he is reported to have died, like the rich man in the Gospel, to whom it was said from authority, This night thy soul shall be required of thee.

During the conquest of Spain by the Moors it was divided into several kingdoms, which naturally weakened its strength, and made them easy captures to the kings of Castille, Aragon, and Navarre, so that the Moors had nothing left in 1238 but the kingdom of Granada. The Arabians, Moors, or Saracens, were

were all the same people, and brought into Spain by Count Julian, as has been already mentioned, whose daughter Roderic ravished, while the father was on an embassy in Africa, where he planned the first invasion by the Moors, and defeat of Roderic the last Gothic king, who was drowned in passing the river Guadatete, whilst flying from the enemy. The kingdoms erected by the Saracens in Spain were, Saragossa by Aben Alfaje; Toledo, founded by Mohammed; Cordova, by Abderrahman; Seville, by Al-Corexi; Valentia, by Zeit Aben Zeit; Granada, by Mohammed Aben Alhamar, who was originally the feeder of a flock, but signalized his valour in so many actions, that he was made a shepherd king in 1238; Cadix submitted to him, and Granada was his capital; he died at thirty-seven, and left two sons. In 1273, he was succeeded by Mohammed Mir, who reigned thirty years, and built the palace of Nugno at Granada.

Mohammed Aben Alhamar came to the crown in 1305, and, after reigning eight years,

years, was imprisoned and killed by his brother. He took some towns during the troubles of Castille, and refused to pay the tribute to its king, which had been always exacted from the Moorish monarchs; he held a synod, and allowed the clergy to keep mistresses. He lost his eyes by an accident just before his imprisonment and murder.

The fourth king, Mohammed Aben Azer, having killed and taken possession, was dethroned by his subjects, who conspired with several Moorish governors against him, four months after his accession.

Ismael, the fifth king, in 1314, shared the same fate, though he had laid siege to Gibraltar without taking it, but had defeated the Christians in a pitched battle, and made two of their generals prisoners.

Mohammed, the sixth monarch, came next in 1328, a youth, and under tutors, who involved him in a war with the Castillians, in which he was beat, and saddled with a tribute of 120,000 doublons. The king of Castille then

then presented him with a splendid robe, and his subjects deposed him for accepting it.

Joseph, the youngest brother succeeded in 1334, and under the protection, and with the aid of Miralmumin exempted Granada from the Castillian tribute; but was conspired against by his successor, and put to death in a rebellion of his subjects.

Mohammed Lagus, لغوس the robber, succeeded, and reigned till 1360, when he was driven from the throne in favour of Mohammed Ahmer, the red.

The ninth king was Abenalamar, killed by Don Pedro the Cruel in Seville, whither he had gone to conciliate his favour. He had only reigned two years.

Mohammed Lagus, then called the Old, came back and reigned altogether twenty-two years.

Mohammed of Cadix, son of Mohammed Lagus, succeeded in 1394 and reigned peaceably thirteen years, the only instance of a Moorish Prince of Peace during the whole of his reign. He married the king of Tunis's daughter,

daughter, and was enabled by this connexion, and strong frontier towns in Andalusia to keep his subjects quiet, and himself undisturbed.

Joseph, his son, succeeded in 1409. He was kind to the Christians, and being engaged in foreign and civil wars, his son conspired against him, and the king of Fez, jealous of his clemency to infidels, sent him a poisoned vest of cloth of gold which soon put an end to his existence.

Joseph was his eldest son, but Mohammed Aben Balva mounted the throne to the prejudice of his elder brother in 1412, and after reigning twelve years died peaceably, having conciliated the king of Castille, by paying the ancient tribute, and sending him presents of his most beautiful wives.

Joseph then followed him, who ought to have preceded; he reigned four years, and trod in his brother's steps, and paid the tribute.

Mohammed, his son, called kawes قوس or crook-backed, began to reign in 1428. He was much beloved from without by the

princes,

princes, his neighbours, but hated by his subjects, who drove him to Tunis, and obliged him to abdicate.

Mohammed Kemelee, or the little, قبلي, who headed the rebels, succeeded that same year, but was deposed after twenty-two months reign for his baseness and cruelty.

Mohammed the crook-backed then returned in 1430, but was dethroned by a competitor, set up by the king of Castille, to whom Mohammed refused to pay the accustomed tribute.

Joseph Aben Almah, rival of Mohammed, made himself a vassal to the king of Castille, but died in the sixth month of his reign.

Mohammed Crookback then succeeded again, and after three years was dethroned by his nephew.

Mohammed Lenk, the lame, لنك, having dethroned his uncle, joined those of Navarre against the king of Castille, but was defeated, and afterwards dethroned. He was famed for his cruelty, and forced many of the Moorish knights

knights out of the country. He reigned from 1436 to 1452, when

Aben Ismael removed him. Muley Haffan, the eldeft son of Aben Ismael, invaded Caftille in time of peace, which his father highly difapproved.

Muley Haffan came not himfelf to the throne till 1470, when he conquered part of Andalufia, and plundered the territory of Alcantara, but was here ftopped by the Chriftians, and dethroned for his cruelty to the family of Aben Caraxes, the moft numerous and confiderable in Granada. He finifhed the Alhambra, and dreffed the Alixares in blue and gold *.

Mohammed

---

* Alixeres was a moft magnificent villa, or country houfe, on the banks of the river Xenil. The artift that overlaid it with blue and gold, got a hundred doublons a day, as appears by the epigram in Spanifh,

El Mora que las labrava,
Cien doblas ganava el dia,
Y el dia que no las labrava,
Otras tantas fe perdia.

Each

Mohammed Boabdelin, his son, succeeded him in 1482, having escaped to Cadix, to avoid being put to death by his father, at the instigation of his wife. He was taken prisoner, however, in fighting with the Castillians, when he made such terms with Ferdinand, king of Castille, that he was suffered to be at large; despairing, however, of the fortunes of the Moors, and finding them irretrievably lost, he retired to Africa.

Muley Boabdelin, a diminutive of Abdallah, was chosen in his place in 1485, but his subjects were so much split into parties, that Ferdinand, availing himself of their divisions, besieged and took Granada in 1492; Muley Boabdelin was driven from the throne, and consented to lay down his regal dignity on condition the Moors governed by their own laws, and that he should retain his former rank and

  Each day his work was done,
  He a hundred doublons won,
   Such was Alhambra's cost:
  Alike each passing day,
  He left his work to play,
   He a hundred doublons lost.

dignity. Thus Granada returned to the Christians after the Moors had enjoyed it more than eight hundred years, and as a kingdom two hundred and fifty-four; containing one hundred open towns and one hundred and forty-one cities. Before Ferdinand undertook the final expulsion of the invaders, he sanctified his project by a bull obtained from Sixtus IV. authorising a crusade, or holy war, for the sake of Christ. The queen Isabella attended him in some of his expeditions, and they were both in no small peril at the siege of Malaga, which resisted nobly and made a glorious defence; but at last, the reduction of the walled city of Baça, or Baza, with its castle, in the kingdom of Granada, cost 20,000 men. One of the conditions of the surrender of Granada, cut off from all communication with the country, and all hope of relief, after an eight months' siege, was the liberty of possessing the revenue of certain places in the fertile mountains of Alpujarros, once barren, but brought into cultivation by the Moors. It is true indeed of this people, that however they may be considered as deficient in the indispensable requisites, and essential qualities of a polished nation, humanity, generosity, and mutual sympathy, yet they have been, no doubt, of infinite service to mankind in planing his rough corners, and smoothing his wiry edge by the introduction of the light of learning, in an age of dark ignorance, and by the advancement, as early as the twelfth century, of the science of agriculture higher, in many respects, than it has ever been carried in the present age. It appears from a Manuscript, found in the Escurial, the composition of an Arabian scholar of the twelfth century, discovered in the year 1751, and published in 1802 in French, that the agriculture of all countries was at that time understood in Spain, and the sugar-cane, pistachier, bananier, sesame, and chou-marin, the cotton-tree, and the dry rice that grew without being constantly watered, were there raised, and produced in the greatest abundance; to say nothing of their knowledge of manures and skill in composts. See numbers five and six of the Archives Literaires, in which

which are extracts from the Spanish translation by M. Correa de Serra, now in Bonaparte's service. Improvements in husbandry are sometimes not adopted when they are first suggested, and afterwards, at a very considerable interval, re-introduced as discoveries. For instance, dibbling seed which has produced two bushels of wheat per acre more than by sowing, was proposed by Gerard Plat in Henry the VIIIth's time, and repeated by Fitzherbert, as well as the use of two ploughs in light lands, and both of late brought out as new inventions.

It will be right in this place to say a word more on the driving out of the Moors, and to account for their final expulsion from Spain, notwithstanding the capitulation mentioned above, and the assignment of the vale of Purchena, in the kingdom of Murcia, to the Moorish king with a considerable revenue.

And first, their obstinate adherence to the language, manners, customs, and religion of their ancestors, on which they valued themselves so highly, being the religion of so

many

many and so great empires, that they looked on any thing short of pure theism, as execrable; and on all image worshippers as abominations. This alone made them slow to be converted, and a whole year hardly produced a proselyte. The reason given for getting rid of them in a political view, was indeed somewhat different. It was feared on the part of Spain, that from their vicinity to the Mediterranean and to Barbary, they might easily invite their opposite neighbours to invade the Peninsula; and, if they coolly butchered them, the cry of horror would resound from all quarters, and if they drove so many thousands away, they might expect to see them return with their enemies at their head. There was, therefore, no other way left to be quit of them as enemies, but by conversion, for which purpose the clergy was called upon for their aid and assistance, and double diligence in the pious task; but the monks employed were impatient and soon disgusted, and reported the Moors as stiff-necked and hard-hearted, and to be subdued

by

by violence alone, fit but for flaves, and exile; that the only mode to be adopted was to fend away the parents and baptife the children by force. This advice was rejected as barbarous and abominable, when it was recollected that the Moors in power had fuffered the Chriftians to adore the Crofs, and permitted them the free ufe of their religious worfhip. The violent method was in confequence fufpended for a time. In 1499, Ferdinand and Ifabella finding that the number of converts to Chriftianity among the Moors was very fmall, urged the matter ftrongly to Cardinal Ximenes, their confeffor, and he, by bribes and by flattery, converted fome of the chiefs, and chriftened three thoufand at once in a great fquare, and burnt as many Korans. But the mafs refifted, and the cardinal had recourfe to other means, and committed Zagri, a noble Moor, and a great zealot, to the cuftody of Leoni, one of his chaplains, who fo convinced the Moor by ftripes and imprifonment, that he pretended to be converted, and feigned perfuafion; and when brought before the cardinal to declare his

faith,

faith, he told his eminence, with a forced smile, that his eminence had nothing more to do, to convert the rest of his countrymen, than to commit them to the custody of his eminence's lion; by which he alluded to the name of the chaplain. By arts like these, by the sword, and by inquisitorial terrors, the Moors were partly converted, partly destroyed, and partly forced out of Spain: many of them on paying ten dollars a head were shipped for Barbary; but those, to the amount of two hundred thousand, who wanted the means of enlarging themselves, were driven to baptism, and four thousand were burnt, and thirty thousand converted. So efficacious was the power of the inquisition, to clear Spain of its foreign invaders, that the Sevillians complained to the king that their city was a desert, and that within its jurisdiction there were five thousand empty houses, and proposed to grant his majesty a large sum of money to suppress this dreadful court of inquiry, and put a stop to its ravages, or the whole country would become a wilderness.

D Ferdinand

Ferdinand at first appeared to listen to the plaintiffs, but was soon persuaded by the planner of the inquisition, Thomas de Turrecremata, a Dominican, to turn a deaf ear to the complainants. The Dominican told the king, that if he took money to put down the inquisition he would commit the crime of Judas and sell Christ, and that his majesty's punishment would be the same as that of the Arch-Traitor. The Sultan of Egypt also took up the cause, and threatened the Spaniards at Jerusalem, and every where in his dominions, to treat them as the King of Spain had treated the Moors. In defiance of all this, and the common declaration at the stake, that the sufferer had been forced into Christianity, and did not believe a syllable of it; the system went on all through the reign of Ferdinand and Isabella, and the aversion to Christianity grew stronger and stronger, and the inquisition was more and more detested. The emperor, Charles the Vth, having passed the summer at Granada, in the year 1526, and been magnificently received by the Moors,

was

was presented with a memorial, setting forth the grievances the Moors endured from the judges and the clergy; the emperor appointed visitors to inquire into the nature and truth of the sufferings, who found the complaints to be true; but, at the same time, reported, that scarcely seven Christians were to be found among them after twenty-seven years baptism. This produced a Junta of Court-prelates and Lawyers, who ordered the inquisition to sit at Granada, in terrorem, that the Moors should give up their fashions, language, and religion, and three colleges be appointed for instructing their children in the Christian faith. The emperor abated somewhat of the rigour of this decree for a present of eighty thousand ducats, but afterwards the inquisitors continued to burn them, and Philip the Second renewed the order for a total change in their manners and customs on pain of death, forbad their assembling in numbers, or possessing arms, or places of strength and resistance. The Moors had acquainted the Grand Seignior with all the tyrannies of the Spaniards, and retired to the mountains, from whence they were expelled in 1570, by Don Juan of Auftria, and natural fon of Charles the Vth, after they had been tranflated from Granada, and difperfed all over Caftille. At length, in 1609, their expulfion was agreed upon in Valencia, notwithftanding the rigorous oppofition of the barons; and firft, twenty-eight thoufand were fent to Barbary, and then one hundred and forty thoufand afterwards in different detachments; and the king agreed to the propofal of his clergy, that all above feven years of age fhould be expelled. The barons oppofed them in vain, for the ecclefiaftics preached every where, that it was lawful to put all Moors to the fword, if the king commanded it; and the invincible armada would never have failed if they had been banifhed long before. Thus Spain loft firft and laft from fix to nine hundred thoufand fubjects; and in 1618 a memorial was delivered by the junta to Philip III. which fet forth the dire effects of this mighty depopulation, by fhewing that the country was on the brink of ruin, which

brought

brought on the disgrace of the Duke of Lerma, and the death of his brother, the cardinal of Toledo, who, being banished from the court, died of vexation. With the Moors went all the merchants and the agriculturists of the kingdom, as it were, for they were the great traders and husbandmen of the land. Philip endeavoured to repair this calamity, and replenish the vacuum which it made in the Peninsula, by a most salutary and flattering edict, which offered the honours of nobility to all cultivators of the lands, with an exemption from military service; but the edict made no great sensation, and produced very little effect on a people, one part of which was naturally indolent, and habitually averse to the exertions of manual labour; and like the Sybarites of old, to whom the very idea of toil and fatigue gave a pain in the side, started back at the sight of a spade or pick-axe, whilst the other took no delight in any thing, but the art of war, and gloried only in the traffic of the sword.

REMAINS OF ARABIC
IN THE
SPANISH LANGUAGE.

SPANISH.	ARABIC.	ENGLISH.
Aba	ابا	Abhor, ware.

Aba in Arabic means, abhorring, dreading, bewaring.

Abenuz	ابنوس	Ebony.

The Spaniards have also, Ebano for Ebony.

Abila	ابيل	Grofs ſtaff-pillar.

Abila is a mountain oppoſite to Calpe, and makes with it the Pillars of Hercules. See Pliny, and the Arabian Geographer, Ebn Haukal, p. 24. 4to.

Açacan   سقا   Water-carrier.

Syka and Sawkee, with the article prefixed, are what the Italians call Secchie. Witness, la Secchia Rapita, the Rape of the Bucket by Tassoni.

Açafate   الشفت   Quiver.

Açafate means a flat basket for ladies'-work. Shaft in English, a perpendicular pit. In Arabic a flat couch, and a quiver.

Açafran   زعفران   Zafran   Saffron.

Acelga   سلق   White beet.
           شلقه

Selk and Selka with the article make Acelga.

Acemite   سميد   Fine flower.

Semeed in Arabic is, with the article, Azemite.

Açote   سوط   Sawt   A Scourge.

                                                     Aceña

Aceña اسیا اب A water-mill.

The Spaniards have changed Aseeab into Aceña. N. B. Aseeab is Persian and Arabic.

Acequia اساقیه Canal, trench.

See Açacan above, and Sakeet, or Sakeea.

Açofar صغر Sufr Copper.

Açumbre زنبر A small Boat, or vessel of content.

Zumber is a Persian word, and may possibly be the original of the Spanish measure.

Alarde العرض The Review.

This word should be written Ardh, or Ardd, Ardz, or Ards, as the letters that compose it are, Ain, Ra, Dad.

Albarcoque برقوق Apricock.

This word is both Arabic and Persian.

Albarda

Albarda   برد and بريد   Post horses.

Bestia de albarda, Beast of burden; Albarda is used also for a saddle.

Albarran   البرّان   The Passing, or Past.

A passenger in life without a fixed abode, or certum domicilium. Persian.

Albeytar   بيطار   Farrier.

Beetaur is the pronunciation of this word.

Albihares   عبهر   Narcissus.

This word is spelt, Ain, Ba, Ha, Ra, and pronounced Abher.

Albogue   بوق   Flute or Pipe.

Albuk or book, is a name also given to a man, pleno rimarum, who can keep nothing, but tells all he knows; and on this account he resembles an instrument full of holes.

Albornoz

Albornoz   برنس   Burnus.

A high crowned cap, worn in Spain formerly, and Barbary.

Alboroque   براك   Courage, joy.

Beraki is an animating ejaculation, used in battle and in civil transactions; also in bargains as a fee, or buona mano, to engage customers. It is abridged in Spanish to Oques, which taylors are forbid to receive of tradesmen for bringing customers to their shops.

Albricias   بريك   A Blessing.

Bereek is a kind of dish made of dates and butter, and means abundance. In Spanish it is used to signify a reward for good news.

Alcaçar   حصار   Castle.

Coins are often said to be struck in the hysn, which is the same as the hysar in this place. The Hha of the Arabians is here changed into a ç. The hysn is the arx, or citadel of a town.

Alcaçar,

Alcaçar, Quiver in Barbary is the great castle. Kebeer. كبير.

Alcahueta كوادت Bawd.

Kuwaudet has undergone some alteration in passing into Spain, and appears to have lost a radical letter.

Alcala قلعه Castle.

Killa is a frontier town or fortification, and thence the proper name of several; for instance, Alcala de Heneras-Real-de Guadayra in Andalusia—De Xivert in Valencia, Alcala del Rio, two or three leagues from Seville, up the river on the opposite side.—De los Gazules near Medina Sidonica in Andalusia. Alcala az Ghazee, The castle of the brave.

Alcantara قنطرت Bridge.

The plural is Kintaur, and Kinteret the singular. Alcantarilla is a town in Murcia, Alcantara is in Estremadura, on the Tagus, where a bridge was built by Trajan, six hundred and seventy

venty feet long, twenty-eight feet wide, of six arches, and still remains.

Alcanzia   جاك   Chak.

A chink, or fissure of a money-box.

Alcaravea   كراويا   Carraway seeds.

Kerawia is Persian for carraway-seeds, and written Kerawia and Kerawiet. Carum carvi.

Alcana   خانه   Exchange.

The house of exchange, house of customs. Do Khana, Town-house. Dogana, like Do Khana, lord of the village.

Alcarria   خرگاه   Cottage.

Khergah is a cottage, or moveable Turcoman hut in Persian, also a royal pavillion, felek ishtibah, high like heaven.

Alcarraza   كشاشه   Pinched pitcher.

Khyraushch means a squeeze, and hence a pitcher for cooling water, pinched, or thumbed in the making.

Alcartaz

Alcartaz   قرطاس   Cornet.

Kartas is a paper cornet, or paper rolled round the hand, open at the top, and pinched sharp at the other end, to hold bonbons, or sweetmeats.

Alcavola   قبول   Receiving.

Kebul, receiving, hence Gabella of the Italian, and Cavala of the Spanish.

Alcauci   خار شوك   Thistle.

Khar is thistle, and Shuk a prickly shrub. Shuk mabaurek is Carduus Benedictus. The Spaniards have dropped the last letter of the Arabic.

Alcayata   خيطة   Peg.

Kheetut is pin, or pole, in Arabic. The Spaniards have so changed the words of the Moors, as in some instances to endanger their identity. This may be accounted for in most cases by their writing them as they pronounced them.

Alcayde

Alcayde   قاضي   A Judge.

Kadi or Kazi, a Mayor-kadi sheher, Judge of the city, Kadi lehaujaut, Judge of the wants of men; this is a name given to God. Kadi asker Judge of the army, a General of an army.

Alcoba   قبة   Alcove.

Kubbeh is an arch or vault.

Alcofa   كوفة   Basket.

Koofeh is a basket in Persian. And in Arabic a round mound of sand, like a turban, and the city of Kufa in Chaldæa. The Arabic proverb, I believe, has been mistaken by the Lexicographers when they render it ليست به توفة و لا كوفة leesa ba tufet, waw la kufet. "There is no vice in him." The meaning as I take it is, "He has neither cap nor tuft," nec cufa, nec tufa. Salmasius, who has written a long note on cufa and tufa, p. 544. Augustæ Historiæ Script. would have said the same thing, had he known this proverb. From cufa comes coiffe, and from tufa tuft.

See

See Meninfki, and Richardfon in كوفه kufa.— Tawfet is excefs, or overtopping, as a tuft does a cap.

Alcohol   كحل   Powder of Antimony.

Kehel is a collyrium for colouring the eyebrows.

Alcorça   خرس   Lozenge.

Khers is a delicacy, fuch as meat prepared for a marriage.

Alcrebite   كبريت   Sulphur.

Kibreet is fulphur; Kibreet ahmer the Philofopher's ftone, or red fulphur.

Alcuña or Alcurnia   قورنده   Family, race.

Khorundeh or Alcurndeh is, with the omiffion of the Dal or D, the correfponding word in Arabic to the Spanifh, and means the family, by way of diftinction, as firnames are wont to be noted on account of fome great and excellent quality, as Guzman el bueno a title given him for his defence of Tarifa in Andalufia.

Alcuza

Alcuza   قزان   Oil-pot.

Kazan is an oil-jar if you will, or a pot, or cauldron in Persian.

Alcuzcuz   اسقسة   A Paste of flower and honey.

Aldava   باب قد   Knocker of a door.

Aldek bab has been altered into Aldaba, and so changed that the Moors could not know them again. Di boni quid hoc morbi est? adeone verba immutarier ex barbarie, ut non cognoscas eadem esse. Ter. Eunuch. 2. 1. 19.

Aldea   دە   Village.

Deh is a town or village. The Persians call a great man, Deh khoda, Lord of the village.

Addiza   دسة   Small sticks.

Desé are two slender bits of wood, belonging to a loom. The Moors gave this name to the brush-wood in Spain about Toledo.

Alheli   جلي   Violet.

Helec is a herb, going out of flower. Alheli, y Alfaqui tanto por el al primero, como por el I en que acaban, son conocidos por Aravigos. Alheli, and Alfaqui, are known to be Arabic, as well by the Al prefixed, as by the final I. Don Quixote, part. iv. lib. viii. c. lxvii.

Alerz   ارسا   Cedar.

Urs or Urus is the Earth or Cypress-tree. See Ezekiel de Erez. c. xxxi. and Arboretum Ursini, vol. i. p. 286. Erez is the general Hebrew name for all cone-bearing trees.

Alexixa   اخبيخة   Sort of Sausage.

Akheekhet is properly a paste of flour and butter, or flour and oil.

Alfahar   فخار   Potter's clay.

Fekhar means Potter's clay, or earthen vessels and also boasting, glorying, which is an attribute of man, who is but clay in the hand of

the

the Potter. The Spaniards call the shop where the potter works, Alfahar. In this word the Kha of the Arabians is changed into the Hha, and in Alcazar the Hha was made a Kha.

Alfajeme   حاجم   Surjeon, or Barber.

Haujem, here the Hha or first letter is made an F.

Alexu   معجون   Confections.

In the Spanish word the M is dropped, and the final N left out, and without the article it is Aju, in which the Ain or A is made F, and the Jim or soft G an X or Kha. Majun signifies kneaded, and an electuary, or confection.

Alfalfa   حلفا   Trefoil grafs.

Helfa is a water herb, to which the Moors or the Spaniards, gave the name of Trefoil, or clover, from its quality of affociation, or growing three together; hence we get the word, in English Help. The F is here again substituted for H. And for Alhulefa we find Alfalfa.

Alfamar

Alfamar   جاموار   Coverlet.

Jamwaur. The F is put for the soft G as well as the H.

Alfaqui   فقيه   Doctor of Laws.

Fukeeh, learned in the laws.

Alfaqueque   فكاك   Liberating a Slave.

Alfaneque   فنوك   Eating up the whole, leaving nothing.

Fanook, a species of hawk.

Alfayata   خياطت   Woman-taylor.

Kheeatut means sewing, from Kheeat a needle.

Alfenique   تنك   Long and Slender.

Tenk or tunuk joined with Nan is thin paste. Here Ta, or T is changed to F.

Aferezia   قراص   The red disease.

نار الغراص nar el feras, St. Anthony's fire.

Alfareck

Alfareek   فراش   Bed.

Ferash is a couch or bed on which you lie. Khesté wa saheb ferash, (he is) sick and keeps his bed. Ferash is also a spreader of carpets and cushions in Persian and Arabic.

Alforja   خرج   Wallet.

Kherj is a cloak, bag, or portmanteau.

Algalia   غاليه   Civet.

This is one of the few words that have undergone little or no change in their transmigration.

Algaña   غنا   Abounding with herbage.

Ghena will mean grass of any sort.

Algarada   غارة   Tumultuary marauding.

Gharet is rapine, plunder, deceit.

Algarbe   غرب — غروب   The West.

A province to the South of Portugal, called Algarve.

Algares   غار   Den, cavity.

Ghar, the socket of the eye.

Alger   زيره   Lime, mortar, zeeré.

Algips   چبسا   Plaster.

Gypsum we have from jibs.

Alguafil   وصيل   Serjeant.

Alwasyl, or weseel.

Alhaja   حاجت   Necessaries.

Hajé, necessaries, furniture.

Alhamar   احمر   Red.

Ahmer, red, barbarous not Arabian. Elah-merani, the two reds, Wine and Flesh.

Alhambra   هم برا   Care, free.

Hem bera, sans souci, is the true interpretation of the name of the castle Alhambra, which all travellers have mistaken by interpreting it red castle

castle from its colour, and leaving out the Ba or B, which makes it حمرا hemra red.

Alhanduque   خندق   A ditch round, a fortified.

Alkhendek is a part of the city of Toledo, lying between hills in a hollow called Alhanduk.

Alhelga   كلع   Fissure in the feet, the space between the teeth not closed.

Alhelga. To produce this word the Kef or second K of the Arabians is softened to an H, and the Ain or A is aspirated.

Alhena   حنا   A dye from a plant.

Hynna dyes the fingers of a beautiful flesh red. The rosy fingered morn we read of in Homer is, perhaps, from Lawsonia inermis, or Egyptian privet. The Spinosa afforded a yellow die for the nails of the Mummies.

Alholbas   حلبه   Fenugreek.

Helebet are milky herbs, of which goats are fond,

fond. Helbet is Trigonella, a diadelphous decandrious plant, between Lotus and Medicago of Linnæus.

Alhocigo فستق Pistachio.

Fistec is the word which the Spaniards call hocigo.

Alhonhiga خندك A Shop.

A pit or ditch in the ground, in which a man works at his trade. See Alhanduque.

Alhomra حمرا A Carpet from its colour.

Hemra is red.

Alhori خرة A heap, or pile.

Kheré is a heap of corn, or bricks, in a barn, or subdio, or in a building, sometimes written Alhori.

Alhuzema and Aluzema وزم Pot herbs.

Wezem is a bunch of pot herbs.

Aljafuna

Aljafuna   جفنة   Bason.

Jefnet is a dish or saucer of a large size.

Aljuma   جما   Assembly.

Jema is a large body of people collected together.

Aljamia   جمع   Spanish.

Jemeea, a number of people talking together, a jargon, which the Arabians called Spanish, or gerriconça.

Aljaruz   جرس   A little bell.

Jiris, a bell, either large or small.

Aljava   جعبة   Quiver.

Javet and not java is the Arabic word. Jaba or java is throwing on the ground.

Aliçaçe   اساس   Foundation.

Asas means foundation, asa fu'l loghat is a grammar, asafu'l seeaset ground work of policy.

Alicates

Alicates   لقط   Pliers, pincers.

Leket is, taking up minute substances from the ground.

Aliçeres   اجر   Tile.
Alixar.

Ejur, made icer with the addition of es.

Aljemofao   كمبها بيع   Pedlar.

Kumbeha beea, a buyer of small wares. Kem is pronounced soft, Jemi, and Beha is lost in Beea, which is changed into fao.

Aljifar   الجلفر   Seed, pearl.

At Julfar, a port in the Persian Gulf, was a pearl fishery, which gave the name to this word. The Spaniards asked the Moors, where they got their seed-pearls; the Moors answered, El Julfar.

Aljofayna   جلف   Earthenware.

Jilf is a vessel or jar, a repository. The Lam or L is dropped in both these words.

Aljuba

Aljuba   جبا   A Garment.

Keba is a short Tunick open before, in the Eastern fashion. The Kaf or K is softened into Jim or G.

Almacan   المكان   Almakaun. The place is a town in Castille.

Almagro   مغر   Acid.

Meker means sour, a name which the Moors gave Almagro in Castille near Calatrava, and Ciudad Real, on account of hard water that was unfit for use, because it had an acid in it combined with an absorbent earth.

Almalafu   ملف   Veil.

Muleff, is a blanket or any thing in which you wrap yourself up going to sleep.

Almanaque   المهنور   The New Month.

Almanack has been variously derived. See Johnson. But most frequently from two languages,

guages, which is inadmiſſible. The Britiſh Encyclopediſts ſay poſitively, that it comes from Al and Manach, a diary in Arabic; without ſhewing that Manach is Arabic for Diary. In this obſcurity and unaſcertained ſtate of the word, I venture to ſay, that Almanach came originally from Al-mah nu, or new month, that is, the firſt month of the year in the Perſian language, in which we have Maheenet, monthly.

Almandarahe ‏مينا دريا‎ Harbour of the ſea.

Meena dereea is Arabic in the firſt word, and Perſian in the ſecond; as in Dereea muheet, the ſea ſurrounding, or all around; Dereea is Perſian and Muheet Arabic, both together are a phraſe for the Ocean, or immenſe ſea; Binihaeet, interminable.

Una eſt immenſi Cœrula forma maris. Ovɪᴅ.

Almaxia ‏مخيوط‎ Garment.

Mekheeut is ſewed, not wove in one piece, like the hauks, or hakes of Barbary.

Almazen ‏مخزن‎ A Store-houſe.

Mekhzen is a magazine.

Almaden

Almaden معدن Mine.

Madin alfezl u'l Kelam, a mine of excellence and oratory, or oratorical excellence.

Almena منار Tower or battlement.

Menar is a turret, and from this word the Spaniards may have got Almena with the loss of the last letter: the proof of this lies in the next word but one, Almenara, a beacon. Abraha, king of Arabia Felix, was called Zu'lmenar, from having first erected beacons, as direction posts, for his return from uninhabited districts, through which he passed to wage war. Minaur and Minaret are this word differently spelt, as the turret of the Mosque.

Almotoli مهل An Oil-pot.

Mohul is the mother or dregs of oil, from which may have been made Motoli and Motolia.

Almiscle مسك Musk.

Galeeat musk, is civet musk; and musk sabunec, musky soap-ball.

Almivar

Almivar ما ابر Juice of preserved fruit.

Ma aber is juice of confections, or fruit preserved by sugar. The two words are made one in Spanish.

Almocaden مقادة Led.

Mekadet means led, conducted; hence a captain, or leader.

Almoçafre زافرة A Dibble.

Zafiret is properly the tip of the arrow, and Mozafiret the same. So long ago as Henry the VIIIth's time, Gerard Platt proposed improvements in husbandry which were repeated by Fitzherbert, such as dibbling the seed, and using two ploughs in light lands, and many others now brought forward as discoveries, though, by the practice of the Arabians, they are no more so now than they were then.

Almocrebe, éve مقرعة Mule-driver.

Mukra-at is a whip, or scourge, with which the mule may be driven.

Almofia

Almofia مغبية Any thing hollowed out.

Meseeat a bason, a recess, or alcove.

Almofrez مغرج A Case, large, open.

Mesrij, or muserej, a case like a pillow.

Almogavares مغاور Marauders.

A houseman, who runs here and there for forage and plunder, in Arabic Mughawur.

Almohaça الباحسه Curry-comb.

From Hesse, to wipe the dust from a horse, to curry and dress cattle.

Almohada مقدم Corner.

Amak and Mukdem are both corners, from whence this word seems to come, by a change, as in the preceding, of K into H. The latter means a pillow in Spanish, and in Arabic the part of the head projecting between the ears.

Almohino مهن Vexing, fretting.

Almojarra جرة Earthen pitcher.

Jarreh is a jar with a great belly, and called also Alcariafa. Carafe is French, and both Arabic and Persian. خزف Khezef by the change of Z into Ra.

Almud مد Half a bushel.

Mudd, a measure, whence the custom house at Valencia, where all the corn is sold, is called Almudi.

Almuerço مورض Breakfast.

Muryz is fasting rigidly, which the Spaniards use to signify the breaking of it, or the conclusion.

Aloja لواص Mead made of honey.

Luwas, pronounced Aloha.

Aloque

Aloque   خلاط   Pale wine, neither white nor red.

Aloque is said to be from the Arabic Halaque, a mixture. Khylaut is a mixture, which, by softening the Kha will be Halaut not Halaque.

Alpuxarras   بوار   Uncultivated mountains.

The Albujarras are a great chain of hills in the kingdom of Granada, seventeen leagues long and twenty wide, difficult of access, unproductive, and barren, for want of cultivation, as the name imports; but now fruitful, owing to the industry of the Moors that turned Christians, and have inhabited them since the expulsion.

Alquerme   قرمزي   Grains of the Scarlet Oak.

The Kermes, or Coccus Ilicis, abounds in many parts of Spain towards Alicant and Valencia, in Murcia, Seville, la Mancha, and in Serranias de Cuença. Women are employed to gather the Kermes, who let their nails grow for the purpose of picking it with greater facility. The

F   French

French word Cramoisy, is nearest the Arabic term.

Alquiler   كرا   Hire.

Kira, is also the origin of our English word, Hire, from the Arabic through the Saxon, Hyran.

Alquimia   كيميا   Alchymy.

Kemeea. The true chymistry is tener renta, to have an estate, y no gastar nada, and spend nothing, which, whoever has and does, will be sure to get the philosopher's stone and grow rich.

Alembique   انبيق   A Still.

Anbeek is pronounced Ambeek.

Alquitira   كتيرة   Gum Tragacanth.

Kuteereh, is Gum Tragacanth, and Kutré petré, Gum Arabic.

Alquitran   كتران   Liquid Pitch.

Ketran, in Persian, is Naptha, a liquid sub-
          stance

stance flowing out of the earth, used instead of pitch or tar. See springs of it in Persia, on the Caspian, in Calabria, Sicily, Modena, and America. It is oftentimes colourless, always highly inflammable, odoriferous, and oily; specific gravity from 0,708 to 0,847.

Altaque   تنک   A Wicker Basket.

Tenk, and not Taque, is the Arabic word.

Alfanega   بنقة   A Net for women's hair.

Bincket, means the opening of a bag, or sack.

Alvanil   بنا   A Mason, or Builder.

Binna, is a Builder; and Kargera, Labourer, and Mamar, an Architect. Alvanil is a diminutive of Albinna.

Alveria   ورکاه   Pool, or Pond.

Wergah, a Pond.

Alvendera   فند   A Gossiping, Rambling Woman.

Fend, may be the root of this word, and it means, Vain words, trifles, age, nonsense, &c.

Albaquia باقي Residue.

Bakee, in the conclusion of letters, is, as to the rest We's'salem, farewell; or Bakee weddua, and with this adieu.

Almanza منزع Foundation, Level, Plain.

A village in New Castille, at the extremity of a vast plain, famous for a victory, which fixed Philip V. firmly on the throne of Spain.

Alhurreca رغايت Foam of the Sea.

Rughaeeut, is also the salt froth that exudes from the roots of canes.

Alhorre پريون Tetter.

Pureeun, is a running tetter, or ring-worm, a disease of the nails, from Purre is Horre, and the last syllable dropped.

Alquaquengi ككنكي Cockle.

Alkekengi, is the Winter Cherry in Tournefort, and the trivial of Physalis in Linnæus.

Kengi

Kengi in Persian is Dumbness, which this plant perhaps produces, equally with the Solanum Maximum, and Somniferum, of the French botanists. The name of Cockle, or Coqueret, is given to it from the whirls of its fruit, Fructu parvo verticillato.

Anacala نان خلع Drawing out Bread.

Anacala is a name given to an oven-drawer, and to the board on which the bread is laid. From Nan khela, nacala has most probably been made.

Anagaga ناي غاغا A Bird-call.

Ghaga is the cry of a bird, which the pipe imitates. Here are two words ناي naee and غاغا ghaga, which mean the pipe-call, and are united in Spanish, and make one by prefixing an A, as in the preceding word.

Anafilar ناي فلار Hautboy.

Naee filar, two words not compounded, but signifying a pipe of a reed.

Anoria   انار   Wells.

Abaur is the plural of Beer, of which Anoria has been made to signify a wheel at a well, for pots to draw up water, as in Norden's plate.

Anzel   امثال   Decree, or decision of wise men, by way of sentence, verse, or saying, worthy of repetition.

Imsal means, beside other things, an order to punish; by way of example, Imsool, also is a wise sentence.

Arrabal   البلد   City, Suburb.

Albeled, a town, or district. The last radical is left out.

Arramblado   رمل   Gravelled.

Reml, is sand, or gravel, on which the Eastern nations write; a particular sort is used by the Arabians, called Ulm u'l reml, science of the sand, on which they teach their children to write, and they themselves draw figures and diagrams,

agrams, cast nativities, foretell future events, and pretend to prophecy.

Arroz ارز Rice.

Arrabon ערבון Pledge, Pawn.

Arrha Arrabon, is Hebrew. See Gen. xxxviii. 17.

Arracadas رخ Cheek-ornaments.

Rukh, a Cheek, decorations of the cheek are pendants of the ear and the nose.

Arracife رضراض Causeway.

A road paved with pebbles. Rezraz.

Araex ريسا Master, of a vessel.

Reesa jehause, Captain of a ship.

Ataud اطب Coffin.

Atud, is a wooden box. Tabut, is also a coffin; and our word Kefen means, in Arabic, dead clothes, and a winding-sheet.

Aximenes اسمان Sunny place.

Asuman is Heaven, which is here put for a warm sunny place, by the addition of a Spanish termination.

Aximeses الاخصام Projecting extremities that overhang a house.

Akhsam, are eaves of a house in Spanish. Observe, that in Aximenes the X is an S, and in Axmeses the same letter is Kh.

Axufayna إسفالن Earthen ware.

Asufaln, is a potter's vessel, or bason of baked earth. The Spanish word ends in Fayna.

Azaleia ازالت A Towel.

Azalet means wiping, effacing.

Azar ازهار Orange-flower.

Azar is flowers. Azhar desté in Persian is a nosegay.

Azaur

Azaur   ازار   Misfortune.

Azarcon   صرفان   Lead.

Surfaun, lead, is Zarcon with an A prefixed, the F changed to a C, and called Red lead, which is another word beginning not with a Sad, but a Seen, a different sort of S. Surenj.

Azavache   شبه   Jet.

Shubuh has been changed into Azavache, by making the Sh a Z, and prefixing an A, and turning the B into a V, and He or H into Che.

Azarote   عنزروت   Sarcocolla.

Anzuroot is exactly the Gum Sarcocolla, being an Arabic term for a Persian gum, or balsam, said to be excellent for the closing of wounds, whence its name Flesh-glue.

Azemila   شملة   Baggage Mule.

Shimillet is a camel.

Azero   زردچول   Steel.

Zerdchul is Steel in Persian, and Zerd is in

Arabic

Arabic a Coat of Mail, from which, perhaps, the Spanish may be derived.

Aziago   ازيغ   Unluckily.

Azeegh is Melancholic, from chagrin and misfortune.

Azicates   ايزاق   Spurs.

Aeezak means, causing to spring forward, expressed Azic with Ates added to it.

Azogue   زيبق   Quick-silver.

Zeebuk is Quickfilver.

Azogue   ازوقه   Market.

Azukeh, signifies Provisions, victuals exposed to sale.

B.

BORGEGUI   برزغه   Buskin.

Borzeghé, is also a Skin, or Pannel-cloth to ride on by way of saddle, from Panneau in French, Cet âne a ni selle, ni panneau.

Barragan

Barragan   بكار   Batchelor.

Bekar is an unmarried person, from which, by inversion, Barrag is formed instead of Bagar.

Bellota   بلوط   Acorn.

Bellut is an Acorn and an Oak. Shabellut, the Royal Oak.

Benalaque   بنا لخ   Farm-house in a vineyard.

Bina lukh, a building of cane, a cottage, or lodge in a vineyard, during vintage-time, called in Persian Sepenj, a lodge for those who watch fields. See Isaiah i. 8.

Borrah   براح   Striking out, effacing.

Berah means ending, finishing, and here Borrah is, to cause to be no more, by blotting out and erasing.

Balcon

Balcon   بالاخانه   Balcon.

Balakhauneh is a Gallery, or Balcony at the top of the house. Balakhauneh wizaret means, the Balcon Vizeer, or head minister.

C.

Caçador de Alforja. See Alforja, in its place, the hunter of the wallet.

Cadillos   גדלים   Fringes.

The shaggy end of any thing wove, is in Hebrew Gudilim. See Deuteronomy xxii. 12. and Instita in Latin, a border, and 1 Kings vii. 17.

Cafila   قافلت   Caravan.

Zaferia   زفر   Village, or Collection of People.

Kaufilut, a company of travellers. The Chief of a Caravan, Kaufilut basha.

Cafio خانه   Not Speaking (Arabic).

Khafet, is ceasing to speak, rude and unpolished in language.

Zagal شخل   A Boy.

Zagal is a Postboy, and in Arabic, Shekhel. Leur ardeur (des mules) se rallentit-elle, le zagal, qui est comme son postillon, s'elance du brancard, les anime de la voix, et du fouet. p. 3. v. 1. ed. ult. Bourgoing.

Zaguan زازرك   A Porch, or Vestibule.

Sazak has been altered into Zaguan apparently, as there is no other word that I know in Arabic or Persian, beginning with ça for an entry to a house.

Zahinas ضیان   Sops of Bread, Honey and Water.

Zeeaun is Honey mixed with water. The power and sound of ظ, or Da in Arabic, is Dth which the Spaniards represent by Za.

Chiz

Cahiz قياس A Measure.

Keeaus contains, in some places, twelve, in others eight, in others six Spanish bushels, or hanegas.

Zahon اشم Breeches.

Ashum without the A, is Shum, which has been made Shon.

Zahor زهر Whiteness.

Zehr means whiteness, beauty, a flower.

Zahouri زهو A lie.

Zuhou means a cheat, a lie, of which Zahouri has been made.

Zalea شال Coarse-mantle.

Shal is a furred cloak, a sheep's skin with wool on it; one also of wool and goat's hair, worn by Dervises, one also made of silk and camel's hair.

Calipha

Calipha   خالغ   A Vicar.

Abubeker succeeded Mohammed, called himself, Vicar of the Prophet of God, Khalif.

Camboa   شمسه   A Citron.

The Spanish word should be Zansoa. The Persian is Shemsé.

Zanahoria   شوندر   Carrot.

Shoonder is Zanhor, with the Spanish termination.

Canja   کنده   Foundations.

Kundé is an excavation. The

Caputa   چاپاتان   Slipper.

Chapatan is a boot in Persian.

Zaparron   شتاب بران   Hard rain, falling quick and hastily.

Shitaub baraun has been made Zabaraun, or Zaparron, by dropping half of the first word.

Carça   خار   Briar.

Khar, a bramble.

Carmesi   قرمزي   Crimson.

Kirmozee.

Cenid   سمت   Zenith.

Semt is the Zenith, the point in the heavens directly over our heads, and اصبت the Azimuth, or the path. In astronomy it is the Arch of the Horizon, intercepted between the meridian of the azimuth, or vertical circle passing through the centre of the object, which is equal to the angle of the Zenith formed by the meridian and vertical circle.

Chinela   چنك   Toe of a Slipper.

Chenki muz is the toe of a slipper much used in the house in Spain, called also Paucheleh.

Cid   سيد   Lord, or Commander.

Seed was the name given by the Moors to the famous Spanish general, Roderic Diaz de Bivar, and the Spaniards called him El Cid Ruy Diaz. Ruy is short for Roderic.

D.

Dados   دد   Dice.

Dedd means playing with dice, or cubes.

E.

Enero   ينار   January.

Yeenaur, January.

F.

Fulano   فلانة   Such a one.

The name of any unknown person. He, Monsieur, chose, what d'ye call him. This word in the Spanish dictionaries is called Feloni; Hebrew, which is Peloni; but the Spanish word is is what the Moors brought into the country, and not the Jews. The only difference between the two terms is in pronunciation, in which the Spanish Fulano accords best with the Arabic.

G.

Gibraltar   جبلو الطرك   Gibraltar.

Gebelu'l Tarek, the mountain of Tarek, where the first Saracen Tarek landed, in his descent upon Spain from the opposite shore, in the year 710.

Gineta   قنات   A Cane Spear.

Kenat, a Cane.

Guada   وادي   Channel of a River.

Wadee.

Guadafion   وادي اب   Passage of the Waters.

Wadee Abi. Guadafion is a river in Castille.

Guadahenar

Guadahenar   وادي مينا   Water of the Haven, or Port.

Wadee meena, or Mouth of the river.

Guadajor   وادي چهار   The river of Walnuts in Andalusia, near Cordova.

Wadee chuhaur, the river of four kernels; the word Meghz is left out. The walnut is divisible into quarters.

Guadaira   وادي ارحا   River of Mills in Andalusia.

Arha is the plural of Reha, a Mill.

Guadaladiar   وادي دار   River of Houses.

Wadee'ldar is in Andalusia.

Guadalaxara   وادي خارا   River of Stones.

Wadee'lchara, a city in Castille, on the banks of the Henares.

Guadalbarro   وادي باره   River of Bounds.

Baré is walls, ramparts, trench, palisade, and Guadalbarro, small river, running down the Sierra Morena.

Guadalbullon   وادي بول   River of Daggers.

Bul or bul is a nose, or a pointed instrument; Guadalbullon is in the province of Jaen in Andalusia.

Guadalbunar   وادي بونجار   River of a Field of Battle.

Wadee Bunjar or Bulhar, means also a place where plenipotentiaries meet to settle a treaty, or a truce.

Guadalcana   وادي خان   The River of Recreation.

Wadee khan is a river and a town in Andalusia of reception for travellers, like a caravanserai.

Guadalerce

Guadalerce   وادي حرس   River of Guard.

Wadee hers is a river of protection, or frontier-guard in Granada, called also Guadalhorze.

Guadalertin   وادي تيره   Muddy River.

Wadee teereh in Andalusia, with the insertion of the article, as in the other words beginning with Guada, has been changed from altereh into alerteh, and finally ertin.

Guadaleste   وادي استنان   River of Turnips.

Wadee astan is a river of roots in Granada.

Guadalete   A River in Andalusia, called Lethe by the Romans, to which the Moors prefixed Guada, or Wadee.

Guadalhorra   غار   River of the Laurel.

Wadee ghar is a river on whose banks laurels grow in Andalusia.

Guadalimar   احمر   The Red River.

Ahmer is red: the Guadalimar falls into the Guadalquivir.

Guadalmallete   مهالك   River of dangerous holes, or places.

Mehalk is the plural of mehliket, called corruptedly Mallete. The Guadalmallete runs from the Sierra Morena into the Guadalquivir.

Guadalmedina   مدينة   River of the City.

Guadalmedina, in Andalusia, falls into the sea near Malaga.

Guadalmelera   ميراث   River of Inheritance.

Guadalmelera was once, and should be again Guadalmeiera. The Arabic word is Meeras, Guadalmeeras is a river in Andalusia.

Guadalquiton   قط   River of the Cat.

Guadalket is in the bishopric of Guadix, in Andalusia.

Guadalquivir

Guadalquivir   كبير   The great River.

Guadalkebeer falls into the sea five leagues below Seville.

Guadamecil   مصلال   River in Andalusia.

Guadamecil or mislaul is the river of hangings, that is, where gilt leather for hangings, or other uses is made.

Guadarama   رمل   Sandy River.

The Pass of Guadarama, is situated at the top of the mountain, at whose foot is the town, nine leagues from Madrid. Properly Guadareml or sandy river.

Guadarranque   رماك   River of Mares.

Guadarimak, Mares. The river is in the bishopric of Cadix.

Guaderriza   رصاص   River of Lead.

Guadaresas in the kingdom of Jaen. Resas is tin, and lead; and the former was called white tin, and lead black tin.

Guadarroman   رمان   River of Pomegranates.

Rummaun, is the Pomegranate, and the river in the province of Andalusia, and diocese of Cordova.

Guedaxira   شراحي   River of much Meat.

Sherahee means meat. The Guadaxira is in the province of Estremadura.

Guadazanon   شوي   River of Bathing.

Shuee, washing. Za stands for shu, as we have seen in Zagal put for Shekhel. The Guadazanon is in the diocese of Cuença, and kingdom of Castille.

Guadazelete   زلات   River of Prayers.

Zellat means errors, sins. Zellat u khetaeea, slips, and offences, which beget prayers. Guadazelete is a river in the archbishopric of Toledo.

Guadacenas

Guadacenas   زيب   River of Wolves.

Heeb, or Zeeb, is a wolf, and probably the word should be Guadacebes in the bishopric of Jaen, in Andalusia.

Guadiaro.   See Guadalaviar, River of Houses.

H.

Horra   حر   Free.

Hyr is free, having been a slave.

J.

Jarro   جرّ   Jar.

Jarré is a pitcher. Dar besos, y besitos al jarro, to kiss the jar often, as in Persian, Bus daden; and Na dar un jarro de agua is a Spanish saying, as in the Roman poet, and the Gospel; not to give the smallest favour to any one, even a cup of cold water. Juvenal accuses the Jews of shewing none but Jews the way to the well. Sat. xiv. 104. Matt. x. 42.

Jorro

Jorro   جر   Drawing along.

Llevar la nave a jorro, to tow the vessel along; in Arabic is expressed by Jerr, towing the ship.

L.

Loco   لوق   Mad.

Look is folly, stupidity, in Arabic; and Lukhen the moon, in Persian, as if the mad were moon-struck.

Lonja   لبجة   A long Piece, a Slice.

Lumjet, or lunjet, is what we call a lunch, or luncheon, and the Arabians, a whet before dinner. Minshew knew this as far as the Spanish, but nothing of the Arabic original.

M.

Maçorca   مزير   Flax on a Distaff.

Zeer is linum, or flax, and the Spanish word is used for as much as is usually put on a distaff at one time.

Mancebo

Mancebo منسوب A young Man, a Boy, Mensub, relating to man.

Marrido مرد Lean, Macerated, Fallen away. Mered means diffolving, macerating.

Maravedi مرابطين Maravedi. Money of the dynafty Almoravidarum, in Africa and in Spain, of five princes. Abubeker, fon of Omar, was the firft, 1056.

N.

Naypes نيغ Playing-cards.

Neef is excefs, furplus; numbers from one to three, and three to ten. Vide Gigæi Lexicon, et Caftelli. From Nips in Spanifh, come Pips in Englifh, or numbers of the cards. This is a clear proof that cards are of Arabian invention*.

---

* The word Fifh for counters comes from Pice, of which eighty go to a rupee. See L'Abbé de la Rive fur l'Invention des Cartes à Jouer, 1780, à Paris, who fays N. P. are the initials of Nicolo Pepin, who invented cards. See alfo Diccionario de la Lengua Caftellana, 1734; and Preface to the Conformity of Oriental Languages. Ma fifh is no money, and Pifhadet, in Perfian, before hand, means ready money.

Naranja

Naranja   نارنج   Orange.

Narenj, an orange, Narengee of an orange colour, both in Arabic and Persian.

P.

Peon   باي   Foot Soldier.

Pace is a step, which is made by the Peon at Chefs, or Pawn; a Soldier is Sipah.

Q.

Quajur   كجكر   To Thicken, Curdle.

Kejger means a plaifterer, and Kej mortar, or plafter made of lime, fand, and water, thickened to a certain confiftence. Quajar is, however, derived from the Latin, Coagulare, and Quajo Rennet, from Coagulatio; whence comes alfo our Quagmire, not as Johnfon fays, Quafi Quakemire. The Spaniards are conftant in changing the L of the Latins into I confonant, (J,) and the F into H, as in Hijo from Filius, and Hoja from Folium, whilft the Portuguefe retain

the

the Roman F, and say, Fidalgo, not Hidalgo, with their neighbours. The Portuguese change the Roman L into R, in Ingres and Nobres. In Hindostan an Englishman is called after the Portuguese fashion, Ingreez. The Arabian historians of the Cruzades, gave Richard Cœur de Lion, King of England, the name of Angitar. The Portuguese, in changing L into R, only imitate the Romans, who altered the Greek word λείριον into Lilium, and when they Græcised their own language, wrote Latiaris, Parilia, for Latialis and Palilia, and φραγέλλιον for Flagellum. See St. John, c. ii. v. 15. Evang.

Quexigo   وشيج   Wild Ash-tree.

Weshij is not unlike Queshige; whence, as the Spaniards pronounced it, making Sh a guttural, and Waw a Q, Quexigo.

Quilate   خلة   Caract.

Khelt means a caract, in Arabic Kyrat, spelt Kaf, Ra, Alif, Ta, and not Caract, as in all dictionaries. Kyrat is the twenty-fourth part of an

ounce;

ounce; it signifies also a bean or pea-shell, a pod, a husk, or barley corn.

R.

Regaifa   رغب   Cake, Paste, Clay.

Reghf is forming into cakes, or balls; hence regaifa.

Rejo   رجوم   Dart, Javelin.

Rejum is any thing thrown. Throwing stones at a rock in the valley of Mina, is a ceremony performed by the pilgrims at Mecca, to represent the stoning of Lucifer from heaven.

Rafez   رفيض   Low, Left, Rejected.

Rafeedz means left, and rejected, like the Mohammedan sect of Ali, or the Shiites, which prevail in Persia, called by the Turks Heretics, who are themselves adherents and followers of Sonna or tradition. From the Spanish Rafez comes our cant term of Raffish, low, mean.

Rezio

Rezio   رسين   Solid, Hard.

Resees is hard, firm, strong.

SARACENOS   سرق   Saracens.

The Saracens were originally a people who lived by plunder, such as Virgil paints the inhabitants of Nersæ, Semperque recentes convectare juvat prædas, et vivere rapto. Hence the name of Saracen from Serek to steal, or from the region of Arabia, nearest Egypt, called Saraca, according to Stephanus. Seriké kurdun is to rot in Persian, and Serket means by stealth.

Saraças, or Caraças,   زرسا   Crooked pins, or small particles of Gold in Meat to choak People.

Zersaw is a particle, or filing of gold; as to the use said in the dictionary to be made of these pins, nothing is known.

Saratan

Saratan, or Zaratan, سرطان A Crab.

Surutaun is a Crab, and the sign Cancer.

Sarçahan زرسان Resembling Gold Thread.

Zerfan is a striped silk used by the Moors very thin, known to us by the name of Sarcenet. Sericum Saracenicum of Skinner.

Seges سكي Seges, a Spanish Wine.

Segi in Persian means wine, and Segi khané is a tavern, or wine house.

Sarao سراي Ball, or Dancing-room.

Serai, a palace, court, seraglio.

T.

Taça طاس Cup.

Tas is a cup, or porringer; Tas eflak, the cup, or vault of heaven. The form of the heavens is a depressed arch, resembling a shallow cup, or bason for a fountain.

Tafetan

Tafetan تفتة

Tafté is silk twisted in spinning.

Tagarmina تغار   Provisions, a sweet thistle good to eat.

Tagarnillo   The herb fennel giant, Bekhoor miryem in Persian.

Tahon طحان   A Miller.

Tahona طحانه   Horse or Ass-mill.

Tehhan is a miller, or horse working in a mill, and Tehhannet a mill worked by a horse, ass, or camel.

Tahur تاجر   Gamester, Merchant.

Tajir is a merchant, artful, adroit in his business.

Tagar   To Cut and Slash.

Tagar is called Arabic, but it comes from Talea, a cutting, or slip from a branch, or plant,

H   and

and that from ϑάλεια. The Italian and French have Tagliar and Tailler from the same source. Taleæ ferreæ are iron plates, paid for money by the ancient British, and the modern Swedes in copper. Cæsar. Comment. p. 166. v. 1. Var.

Talvina   تلدوم   Thick Water.

Tulhum, water too thick to drink; when thickened with flower and boiled is a hasty pudding, or pudding à la hâte.

Tapar   تبر   To stop a hole, check, restrain.

Thebr, or Thapar, to stop; spelt Tha, Ba, Ra.

Tarbea   تربيع   Square Trencher.

Terbeea is a quadrangular figure—a piece of square wood. Ensan terbeea a quadrangular aspect (of the stars).

Telliz   تليسه   Saddle-cloth.

Telisé is a Persian carpet; Teliset, in Arabic, a sack.

Tia شو Aunt.

Tia is in Italian Zio, an uncle, in Persian Shu is a husband, and both Italian and Spanish are from the last, considering Shu as a relation, or relative, whether father's brother, or mother's.

Tocal توقل High Place; ascending to a Height.

Tookel, or Tawekkul.

Tocino خوک Hog.

Khook is a hog, of which the Spaniards have made Khookino, and Tookino, or Tocino.

Treba طرف Border, Skirt of a Garment.

Tref, or Teref, is a border, or extremity.

V.

Vosaste—Voste استاد Vuestra Merced.

Vosaste is used only by the descendants of the Moors, and the common people in the provinces for Vuestra Merced.

U.

Usted   استاد   Sir.

Asted, or Usted, is master. Usted Yakub, master Jacob, in Persian, which in Spanish is supposed ignorantly to be a contraction of Vuestra Merced.

X.

Xabeba   قصب   A Pipe.

Keseb, a reed.

Xaharro   اخير   Plaster, Cement.

Akheer is what walls are incrusted with.

Xaheris   خراسيا   An Ass-mill.

Kher-aseea, a mill worked by an ass.

Xalmo   خلم   Sack, Saddle.

Khelm is a covering, or what covers the deer, and used by the Moors in Spain for a saddle, or defence, for the back of a horse, mule, or ass.

Xaquimate

Xaquimate شاه مات Check-mate.

Xarave شراب Syrup.

Xarcias ارایش Rigging of a Ship.

Araeesh means the tackle. Kishtee, of a vessel; in general an ornament, or necessary accompaniment.

Xeque شيخ Lord, or Governor.

Sheikh is a man of authority.

Xergon جرزت Straw-bed.

Jurzet is a bundle of straw to lie on.

Xerquerieu جرزخرقه Slaughter-house.

Jerz is cutting up, and Kherka is cattle, the two words are in Spanish put together, and made one.

Z.

Zahorar زخار To Gorge and be full.

Zekhar is full, gorged with meat.

Zambra   زنبر   A Boat.

Zumber, a skiff, yawl; also a Moorish dance.

Zumbar   زنبور   To Buzz, and Hum.

Zumbour is a bee.

Zorro   بیذره   Fraud, Deceit, a Cheat, a cunning Fox.

Beezaré.

Zubia   زاب   Place where Waters meet.

Zab is a fountain, or spring, from water collected in the ground.

Zaquizami   سقف سامي   Exalted Roof, a Place between the Plastering and the Roof.

Sukf samee are two words in Arabic, and mean roof high, or high roof.

REMAINS

REMAINS OF ARABIC

IN THE

PORTUGUESE LANGUAGE.

PREFACE.

THE Portuguese language, like most other modern tongues, is made up of a mixture of Greek, Latin, Arabic, French, and Italian terms. The Romans, during their residence in Spain and Portugal, established themselves and their language with equal success, and the inhabitants continued to speak the Roman purely, even after they had got rid of the conqueror and shaken off his yoke.

To the Romans succeeded the Goths, and during their reign the Latin continued to be used, though it gradually declined, and ceased to be vulgarly spoken about the time it became, in great measure, colloquially extinct in the year five hundred and eighty-seven in Italy. In the eighth century the Moors invaded the Spanish and Portuguese, and changed their ancient idioms, and from that arose the modern language of those nations; that,

that, in procefs of time, has received the polifh and perfection at which it is now arrived: there are ftill many Latin and Greek terms in them, and Arabic words enough to compile a dictionary, as Scaliger long ago obferved, in his letter to Pontanus, p. 489. edit. Elzevir. 1627.

The moft valuable part, perhaps, of thefe fmall etymological tracts is their certainty, and the little obligation they have to hypothefis and conjecture. If, indeed, the Spanifh and Portuguefe words are as different from the Arabic as Jour is from Diurno, and Diner from Digiunar, or Gain from Unus, through Unare, Coadunare, Guadagnar, Gagner, Gain; yet their derivations are as clear and incontrovertible, as will be feen by a flight attention to the changes the Arabic has undergone in its accommodation to the Spanifh and Portuguefe pronunciation, and want of correfponding letters to thofe of the Moorifh alphabet. This will appear to be the cafe in the following examples in Portuguefe: Almofalla, Alfella, Alfeloa, Almofaça, are in

Arabic

Arabic Almahalla, Alhella, Alhelua, Almohaſſa, owing to the choice or neceſſity the Portugueſe were under of changing the Arabic ح Hha or double H, with a ſtrong pectoral aſpiration, into their own F, and ſometimes into an S, as, for Herdun, to write, Sardaõ. In the ſame manner they have converted the Kha خ ſtill more aſpirated, into F; and Alchaſſe, Alchozama, Alchanjar, are become with them Alface, Alfazema, Alfange.

To the guttural Ain ع they have very properly added an A, in Abda a province, Abdallah, a proper name, and Alâcir a vineyard; Aabda, Aabdallah, Aabacir, to diſtinguiſh the Ain from the Alif.

B is changed by the Portugueſe into V in many words borrowed from the Arabians; as, Alvara, Alvaiade, Alverca, Alviçaras, Alvanel, Alvarraa, which in Arabic are, Albara, a ſchedule; Albaiade, a drug; Alberca, a town; Albeſhara, good news; Albennee, a building, and official name; Albarran, a Chibol. The letter B undergoes another change into M, in Albondeca and Barran, which are, in Portugueſe,

Portuguese, Almondega, a forced-meat-ball, and Marran, a little pig.

The letter T is found to be changed into D, in the word Ataud, from Attabut, a box. G is turned into L, in Lezirias, from Gezeeret, an island, and into Z, in Zeduaria, a plant with a purgative root, from Geduar. Z becomes G, in Algeroz, from Alzarub, a water-pipe, and in Girafalte, from Zorofat, the Falcon Girafalte.

S becomes Z, in Zarame, from Solhame, a cloak of the finest wool; and L an R, as in Nobres, and Ingraterra.

The He is changed into F, in Refens, from Rehyn, a pledge or pawn, رهن.

In compliance with an order of the Royal Academy of Lisbon, Fran. Joaō de Sousa, published, in 1789, a lexicon, in which he traced the Arabic language all through the Portuguese, and improved and corrected the works of Duarte Nunes de Leao, the best that had appeared on the origin of the Portuguese language, first in 1630, then in 1781. After Nunes came Manoel de Faria, and Sousa in in his Portuguese Europe, tom. iii. part. iv. cap. 10. but without addition or correction; Faria reduced the number of Arabic words, two hundred and seven in Nunes, to one hundred and six, and gave no reason for so doing. In 1712 followed Bluteau, who derived but few words from the Arabic either, says Joaõ de Sousa, because he knew little himself, or copied those who knew still less of the language of the Moors.

In the year 1790, Joaõ de Sousa copied and translated, at the recommendation of the Royal Academy of Lisbon, the Arabic documents in the royal Archives, relative to the Portuguese History, or at least a selection of such as were of any importance. The title of his book is, Documentos Arabicos para à Historia Portugueza copiados dos Originales da Torre do Tombo com Permissiõn de S. Magestade, è vertidos em Portuguez por Fr. Joaõ de Sousa. These documents consist of letters to and from D. Manoel, king of Portugal.

The first letter is from the governor of Cananore to the king D. Manoel, and begins

with

with all the pomp of the East, "To the great and glorious sovereign, judge, and sultan of exalted height. (The word Mulla, or Mawla, means sometimes Judge, Omnipotent, from whom there is no appeal.) Lord of sea and land, dispenser of all blessings in all places, possessor of the kingdoms of your enemies, monarch of the East and West; in government both good and great, a veteran in war, master of the sword and the pen, of extensive liberality and perfect justice. May God perpetuate your reign for ever and ever." This letter is an answer to one of the kings, and dated November 8, sixth of Moharram, 1503, from the least of the king's servants, Geneegeer Corobe, who had been appointed governor of Cananore by Cotelery, and retained by D. Vasco da Gama with the title of Guazil. Cotelery was the king with whom Vasco da Gama made peace in 1502.

Letter II. is from the same governor to D. Vasco da Gama, viceroy of India, praying him to recommend Geneegeer Corobe to the notice of every Capitano Mor, or commandant,

ant, that shall be sent to Cananore, and to charge them with orders from the king to shew the governor every mark of amity and distinction, May 27, 1503.

Letter III. from D. Manoel to the dwellers in Azamor, in Arabic, by Abdalla Raheiani, Arabic secretary to the king, requiring them to send the usual tribute of the thousand measures of corn, January 22, 1504. From Lisbon, in 1508, D. Manoel sent a fleet against Azamor commanded by D. John de Meneres.

No. IV. is from the Moradores, dwellers of Zafy, to the king D. Manoel, with a long history of grievances against tyrannical rulers and neighbours, to which they were as opposite as animals, that prey one on another, July 2, 1509.

Zafy, Azafia, or Saffia, lies at the bottom of a gulf in the Atlantic, near the mouth of the river Tensift, 85 m. S. W. of Azamor.

No. V. is from Aly Ben Saied to D. M. king of Portugal. The writer complains of D. John de Meneres, who laid on forty ounces,

ounces, equal to ninety reis per ounce, on every man's taxes, without carrying it into the royal account. Ninety reis make four vintins and a half, or five pence nearly.

Aly Ben Saied was governor of the Moors in Azamor.

Letter VI. from Ibraheem, king of Calecut, to D. Manoel, king of Portugal. Manoueel, Sultan of Pertekal.

The purport of the letter is to entreat his majesty to give strict orders to all Portuguese, who shall wish to enter into amity, and be at peace with the men of Calecut, to treat them with mildness, and not use force to obtain contributions which is out of their power to give, August 6, 1509. The address of the the letter is,

الي السلطان العظيم و الملك الكريم دن منويل ادام الله عزه و نفع المسلمين بملكه امين

"To the great sultan and munificent king, Don Manoueel, May God prolong his glory, and make the Mussulmen useful to him. Amen."

Letter

Letter VII. From the principal men of the province of Sharkeea, to Don Manoueel, king of Portugal, and the Algarves, Lord of Ganoua, or Guinea, and the Zeheban, that is, the two gold mines.

This is an anſwer to a letter from the king, praying to enter into a treaty of commerce with his majeſty, and promiſing to be faithful and obedient vaſſals. February 16, 1510.

Salem Ben Omar, who ſigns himſelf Sheikh of the cuſtoms of Sherkeea, was among the head men of the province allied, and tributary to Manoueel.

Letter VIII. From the inhabitants of Meſſe to Don Manoueel, king of Portugal.

"The dwellers in Maſſé in particular, and in general, the old, the men of full age, and ſebecan, young men and boys, to the king of Portugal, their ſovereign, with thanks for the benefits conferred on them, and prayers for future protection againſt their neighbours who laugh them to ſcorn, for living under the government of a Chriſtian; and many are the Moors that ſay, they have taken great pains to sue for the protection of a Christian prince; but it is plain to see, thanks be to God, that they have neither security, respect, nor property. January 7, 1510."

Massé lies between Zafy and Taftan, in the Atlantic. Abderrahman, mentioned in the letter, governed the Moors of Zafy, in the place of Yahya Ben Tafufa. Massa was formerly Temest, and lies at the foot of Aiduacal, a part of Atlas.

Letter IX. From Açan Mobaty to Nuno Fernandes de Ataide. Açan Mobaty was Sheikh of the customs of Abda. Nuno Fernandes was governor of Ataide. November 16, 1511.

Letter X. From Haji Hossein Rakan, king of Calecut, to Don Manoueel, king of Portugal.

Haji Hossein Rakan, was son of Mohammed, king of Calecut, and grandson of Zamorce. Alfonso of Albuquerque had, by his ambassador, made peace with Mohammed at Goa, in 1509. June 17, 1511.

Letter XI. From de Rashed Reken Wasecl

of

of Hormuz, to Don Manoueel, king of Portugal.

"May the odour of sincerity waft with this its sweetest perfume to the magnanimous sovereign, Don Manoueel, whom God has destined to be completely happy.

"After kissing your royal feet, I lay before them the communications I have from Damascus, of the marching of the king of Room (sultan الروم) against the Franks towards Suez, and of the Shah of Persia against Diarbekr, and the total route of the army of the king of Room, in the absence of their monarch. What we most earnestly pray your majesty is, that your majesty will never cease to care for your kingdom of Hormuz." March 27, 1511.

Rashed Reken, was governor of Hormuz, appointed by the chief captain Antonio da Silveira, who succeeded in the magistracy of Shereef the Guarda Mor of the king of Hormuz. See the Chronicle of King Manoueel, Part iii. p. 57. The Chronicle of the king, as quoted here, is referred to constantly by

Sousa in his notes. On Letter III. see part i. cap. 27. On Letter IV. part iii. cap. 12. Letter V. part ii. cap. 27. Letter VI. part i. 40. Letter VIII. part iii. 24. Letter X. part iii. p. 104. N. B. The name of the writer of the letter is in Arabic ركن Reken, but in the Portuguese Zarkam. The Za perhaps has fallen out.

Letter XII.

LAWS.

Punishments and pecuniary mulcts which Yahya Ben Tafufa established for the government of the province of HARRAS. This Sheikh Abu Zacharia Yahya Ben Tafufa Ben Mohammed, whose glory God prolong, is mentioned in the note to the eighth letter, as having been succeeded in his government by Abderrahman, Feb. 3, 1512. This paper is signed by thirty names, Mobarak Ben Omar the first, Mohammed Ben Amlam the last.

Praise be to God alone; that is, one, or the Integer. O louvor seja

seja dado a Deos ſo, which differs widely from ſo a Deos, to God only, as the Portugueſe has it. God is one and whole, the Arabians ſay, and his creatures fractions.

FINES AND PUNISHMENTS.

The robber ſhall pay a fine of ten ounces, (equal to four ſhillings and ſix-pence,) or one one hundred dinheiros, (equal to four ſhillings and ſix-pence.) N. B. An ounce is ninety reis, or five pence, a dinheiro nine reis, of which nine hundred make four ſhillings and ſix-pence, or his hand ſhall be cut off.

REMARK.

Hands are the offending part in robbing and writing. Stubbs and Page loſt their right hands, by a ſtatute of Philip and Mary's reign, for writing and diſperſing ſeditious libels.

II. Whoſoever ſhall ſtrike with a ſtick or a ſtone, ſhall pay two ounces, or twenty dinheiros.

III. Whoſoever ſhall lay hands on another man's money, if he be a debtor, ſhall pay fifty dinheiros; if it be to rob, a hundred.

IV. If any one strike another with the fist, he shall pay two ounces.

V. Whosoever shall cut his brother Mussulman shall pay a fine of two ounces, or twenty dinheiros, and a kubsh (ram) for the wound.

VI. He who shall furnish arms or money to runaway Moors in time of war, shall pay two ounces, or twenty dinheiros, أو ثوب aw sawb, or a tunick.

NOTE.

N. B. The Portuguese version is, Quem armar conversa sobre os Mouros fugitivos, and omits aw sawb. The Arabic is من ذكرهما سلب Who lends a shining sword, or furnishes a fugitive Moor with a cutting sword.

VII. If a woman treat her husband with contumely, she shall pay half an ounce, or five dinheiros, or a sheep.

VIII. If a man inveigh against his wife, and there are witnesses, he shall pay five ounces, or fifty dinheiros, or swear that he had no bad intention.

IX. If

IX. If a man be found in another's house for any treacherous, or dishonest purpose, he shall be fined ten ounces, or one hundred dinheiros.

X. He who commits adultery with the wife of another Moorman, shall pay one hundred dinheiros from his hoard, and over and above his wife shall belong to the injured husband.

XI. The man that goes back to quarrel with another, after he has been condemned by the judge, shall pay twenty dinheiros, or a tunick.

NOTE.

Sawb is a waistcoat reaching down to the knees, which the Moors wear in the fields instead of a shirt.

XII. Whosoever runs away in time of war, his goods shall be sequestered, his house burnt, and he banished from the king's dominions, and out-lawed. His wife shall be paid her portion out of the sequestration, and if any man kill the fugitive, he shall not be punished as a murderer.

XIII. If a man aſks to be paid a debt owed to him, he muſt firſt acquaint the governor of the country, that he may fix a time for the payment, and if the debtor ſhall not pay at the time appointed, the Kaeed of the place ſhall judge him as he may think fit.

NOTE.

Ahmed Ben Elhajé for whoſe government theſe laws were eſtabliſhed, was the Sheikh of the impoſts of Harras, bordering on Ducala, the moſt northern province of Morocco.

Letter XIII. From Mohammed Shah, king of Hormuz, to Don Manoueel, king of Portugal.

The writer prays to be relieved from one half of the tribute of Hormuz, Aug. 27, 1513.

NOTE.

Alphonſo de Albuquerque, who had made peace with Mohammed Shah, adjuſted the tribute Mohammed Shah was to pay yearly, (Vid. Chron. part ii. p. 56.) of ſo many thouſand ſheraſins in gold, ſilver, and copper.

Letter

Letter XIV. From Açan Mobaty, to Nuno Fernandes, of Ataide.

Açan Mobaty was a principal collector of the imposts of Harras. The letter is on the subject of exactions in collecting the tribute, and complaints of oppression. The writer desires Nuno to give the bearer a present, Inaam. This was a regular thing with the Moors, that the bearer of a letter should be paid by the receiver.

Letter XV. From the Shereef Mohammed, king of Fez, to Don Manoueel, king of Portugal.

Mohammed prays, that the vessels he is about to send to Algier and Tunis may be respected by the Portuguese, when they come from the East; he was afraid of his vessels being taken by Vasco Fernandes Cesar, who was then cruising in the streights. Vid. Chron. part iv. cap. 56.

Letter XVI. From the same, on the same subject, to the same. Jan. 30, 1514.

Letter XVII. From the king of Meleendo, to Don Manoueel, king of Portugal.

A monarch

A monarch is described with a thousand brilliant titles, and at the end it is said, "Don Manoueel is he." The king then tells his sovereign a story in the following terms: "Know, Sire, that heretofore there was a man, and his name was Haleem, who was as liberal as he was rich, and never turned away from any petitioner, or excused himself for not granting what he asked. It so happened, that one who wished to try his generosity to the utmost, came to his house. Haleem asked him his business, he answered, I am come for your head. And what good would it do you, replied Haleem, if you had it? There is a king, says the man, in my neighbourhood, who will give me a thousand ducats (deenaran) if I can bring him your head. Upon which Haleem went into an inner room, and having got together a thousand ducats, he stretched out his neck to the man, and said, Take which you will, my head or my money. The man took the money and went away. Your humble servant, Sire, wishes to make this experiment, and asks of a monarch,

narch, who is more fortunate than Alexander, fairer than the moon at full, braver than Cesar, whose favours refresh like the dew of the spring, to look with pity on the people of Meleendo, and shower down his bounty on their necessities." Here the writer exhausts himself in praise of the king, his master, and makes his principal business an after-thought. Sept. 30, 1515.

NOTE.

This is evidently derived from the story of Hatim Tai, so much celebrated for his liberality throughout the East. There has, perhaps, then been some mistake in the name, made by a transcriber, and instead of *Haleem* it should be written *Hatim*. The name is written حليم in the letter. Hatim was one of the Sehabeh or companions of Mohammed.

Letter XIX. From Khashbur Shah, governor of the port of Baruz, to Don Manoueel, king of Portugal.

This letter in the name, and by the order of

of king Azarkam, was written by the governor in the king's name. Azarkam was governor of the Isle of Baruz frontier, and subject to the Isle of Sumatra, whose sovereign was Khashbur Shah. April 9, 1516. The subject is the inhabitants, and their want of protection, who desire to be relieved, and allowed to pay twenty thousand sherafins instead of twenty-five thousand.

Letter XXVI. From Abderrahman Ben Hadu Almaztradee, called by Sousa Haduxa, without the other name.

" Praise be to the one God, and Manoueel, king of Portugal, Ducala, and the Indies; may God add to his victories, and increase his glory. Abderrahman enumerates his services to the king, talks of his having taken for the king thirty duar, or villages, each consisting of fifty, sixty, or a hundred tents, made of platted horse-hair, for which he had not been thanked, or received any answer to his letter announcing it. That he had lost men and cattle in abundance, and had no hope but in the royal countenance and support against the Moors."

Moors." May 6, 1517. Abderrahman lived in the province of Naâmei, and had in his stables more than a thousand horses, with which he waged war with the king of Fez.

N. B. The remaining letters, with a few exceptions, are to D. Joaõ III. from Meer Abanafar Shah, son of Seifeddin, king of Hormuz, Aug. 8, 1523; from the Shereef of Fez, May 26, 1524; and from various persons. From Ebattar, chief of the allied Arabs, who lived in the neighbourhood of Azamor, and collected the tribute paid to the crown of Portugal. N. B. This is the last letter to Joaõ with a date, Nov. 3, 1530.

REMAINS OF ARABIC

IN THE

PORTUGUESE LANGUAGE.

PORTUGUESE.	ARABIC.	ENGLISH.
ABBA, Za Celaſſe		Padre Servo da Trinidade, tres peſſoas. Za is Ethiopic.

This is the Arabic word ثلاثة three, with Abba, father, prefixed. Father, servant of the Trinity.

| Abderrahman | عبدالرحمان | Servant of the merciful. |
| Alcunha Alkenh. | الكنه | Surname, nickname, something, substance of any thing, mode, sum. |

Abuna

Abuna   ابونا   Nostro padre, Our Father.

Abxim   حبسي   Any thing black, an Ethiopian.

Açacalador   اسقل   Burnisher of swords.
Askel.

The word is formed from the Arabic صقل, with the article prefixed, and the Portuguese termination. The Arabic is properly written with a Sſad.

Açafate   السقاطه   Utensil, household furniture, a basket.

Açamo   كمام   Halter, or muzzle.

Acequiat   الساقيه   A Watering, or irrigation, from Seka, and Sekaiet, a man who supplies travellers with water.

Achaque

Achaque   الشاكي   Infirmity; from Shakee,
Axxagui.   which, in the eighth
     conjugation, is to bewail.

Acicate   الشكة   A Spur of one point; from
Axxacate.   Shak, a shoot.

Acipipe   الزبيب   A Bunch of grapes, passa
Azebibe.   da uva.

Acinippo is a town in Hispania Bœtica, now Ronda la Vieja, on whose coins is a bunch of grapes. Acinum is a grape-stone, with which Anacreon is said to have been choked. Plin. l. 7. c. 7.

Açotea   الشطوح   The Ground-plot of a
Assotua.   house; from Satapa, to extend.

Açougue   السوق   Market; from Sawk, a
Assoco.   place where men are collected together. Ahli sawk the market-people.

Açoutar

Açoutar Savata. Sawt.	سوط	To Lash, scourge with a leather thong. Dar pancadas com cordas correas de couro.
Adail Addaleel.	الدليل	Shewing, a participle of the Surd verb دل ensinar o caminho, to shew the way, where the third radical is not heard.
Adarga. Adarâ. Adaga.	ادرع	A Shield of leather, used formerly by the people of Spain and Africa; from Daraâ, to arm; in the eighth conjugation, to arm yourself, and be armed with a passive signification.
Adarme Adderhem.	الدرهم	Forty grains, a coin.

Aduana

Aduana Aldeeuana.	الديوان	Hall of administration of public affairs. Deewan means also an account-book, muster-roll, and military pay-book.
Aldafe Aldef.	الدف	A single drum, with one skin, also a cymbal, tambour de Basque introduced into Spain and Portugal by the Saracens, called Pandeiro by the Portuguese.
Albarrada	البارات	A Clay vessel, or pot, in which flowers are set. Werd, as it is called by the Arabians, is a rose-tree.
Albergate Albalgat.	البلغة	Morocco slippers, Calçado de Marroquin alparcas, Moorish shoes.

Alparcas

Alparcas are made of pack-thread, and sometimes of rushes.

Alborge البرج A Tower. Borjon, for-
Alburj.   tress, or castle.

Albornos الباراني Mequinezes, cloaks
Albaranee.   with hoods and capes for winter wear, made first at Maquinez in Africa.

Alcoree الغرص Sweetmeats in shapes for festivals.

Alçada السادات Princes, Lords, de-
Alsadat.   scendants of Mohammed, Justice.

Alciado السيادت Dominion, govern-
Alseeadet.   ment.

Alcaeed الغايد A President, or general.

Assento

Assento de Madeira السند A Plank of wood,
Assened.   or thin shingle; in
            low Latin, Cen-
            dula; also a prop
            on which another
            leans.

Alanse الحنش
Alhanaxe.

Alardo العرض A Review of soldiers; from
            árada, he appeared.

Alarife العرف Architect; from Arfan,
            knowing, intelligent,
            scientific.

Albafor البخور Incense, perfume in
Albachur.   Persian.

Albalequim البالغين The Age of Pu-
Albalegeen.   berty, fourteen
            for men, and
            twelve for wo-
            men.

men. From ba-
ligh, arrived at,
reached, full,
perfect.

Albarda البارةعة Covering of straw for
Albardaá. beasts of burden.
Bardan means in
Persian, a reposi-
tory for travellers'
goods, and poles
supporting awn-
ings.

Alcatifa القطيفة A carpet, or cloth, with
Alketeefet. a long pile.

Almogaures البغاور A Warrior, and
marauder, one
who makes ex-
cursions to
plunder, and lay
waste. From
Ghar.

Alcuzcz

Alcuzez Alguzar.	الكذار	Somnolency. Khab guzar, sleepy, lethargick, going to sleep. Khaub is left out in Portuguese.
Alfadael Alfadaeel.	النضايل	Liberality, virtues, excellencies.
Alfitra Alfytr.	الغتر	Tribute of the Moor to the king of Portugal. Alms given upon an Aeed, or a grand festival, called Aeed fytr.
Auge Auj.	اوج	Acme of good fortune, the top, or summit. Auj Sheref the fortunate aspect or ascendant of a star.
Alcaçus Arquessus.	عرق السوسا	Root of the plant Sûs, or liquorice.

K 4   Alcanfor

Alcanfor الكافور Camphire. Shama Ka-
Alcafur. fooree, a camphorated
wax-candle.

Adela دالة A Woman that cries goods
for sale in the streets.
From Dalet, becoming
public.

Agoa

Com agoas paſſaos, naõ moe o minho.

The mill cannot grind with water that has
left it. This is also an Arabic proverb:

لا تدوار الرحي لها قد مض

There is no turning of the mill by water below it, or water already paſſed.

Albaraa البران Onion. Buſulu'l faur,
Albaran. wild onion.

Albáraa بري Rude, ruſtic.
Berce.

Alvaſi

Alvasi   القاضي   The Cady, or Judge.
Alcazi.

Arratel   رطل   A pound of twelve ounces.
Retel.

Arremeçar   رمي   To throw from the hand, or he threw (a dart).
Remee.

Azmodeo   ازموده   Tempter. From Azmuden to try, here it is in the paſſive, tempted.
Azmudo.

Até   حتي   Untill. In Spaniſh Haſta, from the ſame word.
Hettee.

Abra   عبر   A Bay, or anchorage for ſhips, differing from a bar, is from âbir, to enter in, and paſs from one ſide to another. Abr is alſo a ſhore, or margin.

Açafraõ

Açafraõ الزعفران Spicery. Abzardan a box
Azzafaran. for spiceries.

Açofifa السيب Alseeb and Alseev, or
 Seef, an apple. Ma-
 çaā de Nafega.

Aҫude السيد Alsedd, or sedd, an ob-
 struction. Sedd Yajouj
 u Majouj, the wall of
 Gog and Magog.

Acafelar تغل Kufl, a lock. To lock up,
 fechar com cadeado
 vossa mulher.

Adibo ذيب Addeeb, a wolf; a thief, in
 German. Dieb from the
 Arabic, so also the Saxon,
 from whence we have it.
 Dau'z zeeb is the wolf's
 disease, or hunger.

Adobe

Adobe	الطوب	Attobi, a species of brick dried in the sun.
Adubo	طوبي	Sweet spiceries. Tubee in Arabic. Addaffa, a lattice. Janella com adufa, from دفة deffet, two boards put together. Deffe'l kitaub the boards of a book.
Alabaō	اللبان	Allabban, ewes full of milk; from Leban, a breast of milk: Akhuo bilibani ummihi, a brother of my mother's milk, i. e. a foster-brother.
Azenha	اسيا	Aseea, a mill. Auseeaub, a water-mill.
Alface Alchasse.	الخسم	A weed, a thistle.

Alfazema

Alfazema Alchozama.	الخزمه	An aromatic plant.
Alfange Alchanjar.	الخنجر	A short broad sword in Turkish.
Almofalla Almahalla.	المهله	A field of battle.
Alfella Alhella.	الحله	An encampment, from Hel, to rest and stay.
Alfeloa Alhelua.	الحلوه	A Sweetmeat.
Almofaça Almohaffa.	المحسه	A Curry-comb.
Azafama Azzahma.	الزحمه	A Crowd. Mecca is called Um Azzahm, mother of the crowd.
Azagaya	الخازقه	Alchazeca, a Moorish lance for cavalry.

BALIQ

B.

Balio   ولي   Presiding over, governing,
Wely.   Senhor principe.

Bedem   بدن   Capa, a cloak, an orna-
Beden.   mental girdle, worn by
    the Arabian ladies. A
    short coat of mail.

Beledulgerid   بلاد الجريد   City of palm-
Beladulgereed.   branches.

Bledeljerrede pronounced.

Beleguins   بلغ   An Officer of justice who
Belegh.   follows, watches, and
    seizes. Belegh, obtain-
    ing, consummating.

Bezuar pedra   باد زهر   Expeller of poison.
Bad zehr.   Bezoar stone, or
    antidote.

Boun

Boun   بن   Coffee berries before roasting. Ograo antes de ſer torrado.

Boſa rinheiro   بوالحنه   A Vender of al-henna, or henna, the dying, colouring herb. Lawſonia inermis. The Arabic word for buying and ſelling is Beea.
Bulhenna.

Buzidan   بوزدان   Root of a herb in India, called Teſticulos da Rapoſa. Fox-ſtones. Aviceña, 95. 110.

Borax   بوراق   Nitre, borax uſed in ſoldering gold, called Burei zergeran. Tinkaur Perſian, whence Tinkal in German.

Badajos

Badajos بلاد العيش Land of support. In
Beladulaeesh. the Nubian Geography it is Badalius, and anciently was so pronounced. It is now a city of Estremadura on the Guadiana.

Bacoro بقار Bekar, cattle, cows of a small breed, a little pig.

Balsamo بلسان The Balsam-tree.
Belesan. Balsam.

Balcam بالاخانه A Balcony.

C.

Câlataynb قلعة ايوب Fortress of Aiub, Job, the Moor who founded it in Arragon. Vid. Geogr. Nubiens.

Cacerben

Cacerben Danes   قصربن دانس   Fortress of the son of Danes, the founder.

N. B. The Moors call their houses after the names of the founders. The Spaniards from the names of the lands, as in France and Scotland.

Caraça   قراك   Kerad, a tike.

Chafaris   شكاريج   Xacarige, a fountain with a spout, or without one.

Cufcus   قسقس   A Cake made of flour and water in Africa.

Caba   كعبه   A Square house, with the article, the Temple at Mecca.

Cava   كحبه   Mulier má, an adultress.
Cabha.

Zala

Zala Selat.	صلاة	A Prayer, benediction. Af-felat arrabeet, The Lord's Prayer.
Ceroulas Serwal.	سروال	Breeches.
Chita Kef.	كف	A Shield of leather for the hand, like a cestus, used by Persian soldiers.
Corgi Baxi Bashee Corjee.	باشي كرجي	Captain of a troop. Basha in Turkish.
Cordovam Cortobanee.	ترطباني	Cordovan. At Cordova was the first fabrick of leather in imitation of Morocco.
Calahorra Calat'lhōra.	قلعة الحجرة	A City of Old Castille. A fort of stones on a hill.

Calatrava

Calatrava   قلعة التراب   A City of New
Calaterab.   Castille, a land
                                fortress.

Zarafo   صراف   A Money-changer.
Serraf.

Chocarreiro   سكرة   Ridiculing, sneering.
Sukhuret.

D.

Dervixe   درويش   Dervise, a religious
Derveish.   monk. Derveishee,
                                poverty.

Debul   دبول   A Calamity, a wound in
                                the lungs. Avicenna,
                                cap. 2. p. 26.

Durazios   دراقن   Derakin duraqueno, a
                                species, or sort of Per-
                                sian peach that is
                                white

white and of delicious flavour.

E.

Elche علج A Proselyte, from one religion to another. A man wavering between two opinions; like a camel, whose pace is, in Arabic, Alejan.
Alej.

Elixir الكسير A Fifth essence; the philosopher's stone. Elikfir doulet, the elixir of fortune.
Alikfeer.

Endivia هندب Endive, succory.
Hendeb.

Enganar خوان A Deceiver, betrayer.
Kawwan.

Pronounced Khan, with En prefixed and Ar added.

F.

Fasquia   فسخيه   Fascheea, a lath; from Faskh, a division, splitting.

Fanfarram Ferfar.   فرفار   Loquacious, boasting.

Fen   فن   Learning, science. Fen achlak, the science of Ethicks.

Frangau Furuj.   فروج   A Chick. Gallo pequeno.

Fulus   فلوس   A Coin, worth half a real, $2\frac{1}{2}$ d.

G.

Gabam Keba.   كبا   A Short tunic open before.

Gafar   غفر   Small Tribute, paid by the Jews and Christians to the Turks.

Garabia

Garabia Gherbee Garbon.	غربي	The West, Western.
Garrama Gheraum.	غرام	Ghereem means a debtor, a prayer of tribute, and Gheram a debt which must be paid.
Gazua Ghizou.	غزو	Making war, an act of convocation to religious war.
Gindi	جندي	A Soldier.
Gota Gout.	كوت	Pains in the feet.
Guadalabiar	وان الابيار	Rio os poços, beeron o poço, a well. Abiar os poços.
Guadelcacer	وان القصر	The River of the palace.

Guadelcaru

Guadelcaru واد الـجاره River of relief, aid, or defence, a city of New Castille built on it.

Charé in Persian has the same meaning as our word Char, assistance of any sort, or time, in performing odd jobs. The Saxon word is the same.

Gudalhanar واد الغانوس The river of the
Guadafanar. Phanos, or Light-house.

Guadelmedina واد المدينه River of the city.

Guadeluppo واد العب Vade lub, a river of New Castille, Rio de Seio, Geograh. Nubiens. river of the bay.

Guadiana واد يانا Passage of the Yana.

Guitarra

Guitam قيتار An instrument of music with four strings. جار تار char tar.

Guita Kheet. خيط Pack-thread.

H.

Hamet احمت Ahmet, proper name of a man.

Hodamo عظام Odamo, something great; from عظم.

Hued el barbar واد البربر Vad el barbar, Rio caudaloso, long-tailed, de Barberia, rising on Mount Atlas and running into the Mediterranean.

Hysopo, Azob الزوف Azzof, a herb.

J.

Jaezes   جهاز   Jehaze, the trappings, arreios, of a horse, hum cavallo.

Janizaro   انكشري   Vox Turca, Anquisaria, a new troop.

Jarra   جرة   Jarra, Jar.

Jasmin   ياسمين   Jasemin.

Javali   جبلي   Jabali, wild mountain hog.

Joia   جوهر   Jauhar, a shining substance.

K.

Kabk   كباك   Kebaq, a partridge, or galena, from the sound it utters of Keback.

Kanisat el Gorab   كنيسة   A congregation of
Algreia do Corvo   الغراب   crows.

Kequenge

Kequenge or Alaquenge كاكنج Cacange Physalis, a Moorish plant.

Alkekenge of Tournefort.

Kiarchamber خيارشنبر Chiarxambar, caña fistula.

Kaçabe قصبه Casabe, where sugar-canes grow. Cannavial de açucar.

L.

Laca لك Lacca, scarlet colour, extracted from the juice of a plant.

Lacaio Lackey. لغي Lekee, a servant, any thing thrown away as worthless.

Laqueca عقيقه Aquica, cornelian, precious stone of a red colour like a garnet, stanching blood.

Larim

Larim لاريم Larim, a Persian coin from the town of Larim, worth sixty reis, 3 d. two-tenths.

Lascarim لسكريم A cavalry soldier.
Lascareem.

Lezirias جزيرات Jazirat, island.

Limao ليمون Laimun, lemon.

Locafa لقحا Lacaha, a company, tribe.

Lofada لفحا Lafaha, a strong gust of wind.

Lohoc لعق Lo óq, from Laâca lamber, to lick.

Luletem لولتيم Luleeteim, two pearls.

M.

MAÇAGAON ماصاخن A place in Africa in the province of Ducala; meaning also stinking water.

Macio

Macio	مسيح	Macio, smooth. From Maçaha, polished.
Madraçal	مدرسة	Madraça. From Daraça, he studied, a school for reading and writing.
Madrid Madrit.	ماجري	Maajreet. From Maajreet, running water, therefore rightly called Madrit.
Magos	مجوس	Majus, Majician, or searcher into mysteries, philosopher.
Mameluco	مملوك	Bought. A purchased slave.
Mancebo	منسوب	Manſubon, an enamoured person.
Mandil	منديل	Mandeel, a hair-cloth, a coarse apron.
Mangil Manchil	مجل	A scythe.

Mar

Mar	مار	Synonimous with Senhor santo, also a Lord, and rich man.
Maracotuon Baracoton Woolly.	براتطن	A yellow peach grafted on a quince tree, woolly on the outside.
Maravedi Marabateen.	مرابطين	People of Arabia, of the sect of Ali, opposed to Omar. From Rabata, firm, compact; which the sect of Omar was not. Maravedi is a word used in reckoning, but no coin.
Marlotu	مرلوطه	A short dress of the Persians and Indians.
Marquezita	مركزة	Pirites in the veins of metals.
Mastica	مصطكا	Mastich, commonly called almeega.

Mafcara مسخرة Scoff and jeſt; from Sachara, in the fourth conjugation.

Matamorra مطمورة Cellar to keep wheat
Matmuro. in; from Tamar, to hide under ground.

Matraca مطرقة A wooden rattle with two iron-rings, uſed to call prieſts to the choir in the holy week.

From Terk, ſtriking a harp or lute. The ancients uſed rings at doors inſtead of knockers, of which Almeloveen has given us a plate, in Conjectanea, p. 150. 12mo. Amſtel. 1685.

"For none but that in honour live ſhall touch my ring."
CHATTERTON.

Matruxibaxi مطرشي باشي Carrier of water in ſkins, or principal water-carrier.

Meſquinho

Mesquinho   مسخن   Poor, indigent.

Mulana   مولانا   Our Lord.

Motrias   مطراس   A site in Sentarem, fourteen miles from Lisbon. Santarem, or Santa Irene. Also a bar, or bolt, across a door. From Turs, a shield, or security.

Mexuar   مشور   An audience chamber, a place of consultation, to deliberate in, where the king gives audience.

N.

NARUZO   نرجس   Narges, narcissus.

Nataf   نطافت   An oily mineral earth affording bitumen, used for burning like pit-coal. From Natafet, shedding, flowing.

Nacar

Nacar نكار Nacar, painting of various colours.

Nora ناعوره Naura, hydraulic machine, used to draw water out of wells, cisterns, rivers.

Noradin نورالدين Nureddin, light of religion.

Nunged نواجد Nauajed, the grinders. Sousa quotes Avicenna, cap. v. p. 11. The word for grinders is, نيوب the plural of ناب naub.

O.

OLEID AHMET وليد احمد Ueleed Ahmed, a family name, a praise worthy child, worthy son. Ahmed is one of the names of Mohammed.

Oquia

Oquia   وتيه   Uakia, an ounce. Twenty ounces of gold make two hundred and forty cruzados.

Oxala   انشا الله   Enxa Allah, may it please God.

P.

PAPAGAIO Bebagha.   ببغاء   Parrot.

Paparras   حب الراس   Habberrás, Seed for the head. An herb called Piolheira, whose seed kills, os piolhos, lice.

Pateo   بطحة   Pathaton.

N. B. Pateo is a court, or yard. From $πάτος$, via calçata, in Greek. Sousa's word Bethet is the stature of a man.

Pato   بط   Batton, a goose, or duck.

Pagoda

Pagoda بت خدا God's image, idol,
Betkhoda. temple.

Pendaō بند Bendor in Persian, a standard with streamers carried in processions.

Pir Beq بربیک Pir bec; a Turkish word of military dignity, of the rank of colonel.

Q.

Quirat قراط Quirat: a carat, a seed of Alfarroba, St. John's bread, six grains of wheat, used by shop keepers.

R.

Rabique راویق Raveek, face-ornament; from Ruc, or Ravac.

Recova	ركوبه	Rocoba, A company of horsemen, an attendant on horsemen. Rekubu'l kousej, the cavalcade of an old man without a beard, in the Persian Masquerade, at the end of winter.
Regucifa	رغيغه	A little loaf with a hole in it, used in the province of Minho. A loaf in the shape of a ring at Oporto.
Resma	رزمه	Resma de papel; from Razama, a ream of paper.
Rihana	ريحانه	Reehana, a garden, an odoriferous herb.
Robe	رب	Fruit boiled to the consistence of honey.
Roca	روقه	Roca, (rock,) a distaff for spinning thread, or wool, and cotton.

Romaã

Romaā	رمان	Rumman, the pomegranate. Rummani, like a pomegranate. Rummauyet, a dish dressed with the seeds and juice of pomegranates.

S.

Saca	ساكه	A duty for goods embarked.
Safena	سافين	A vein of the knee divided into three branches.
Saffo	سفلي	Saflio, the skin of a conger, or like it; is derived from Seflon, a bottom, or low place.
Sagapejo, or Sagapeno	سكبينج	A sort of gum much used in the shops.
Sagres	سغر	Sacron, a piece of artillery so called.

Saguā

Saguaõ, Xaquaõ   صجن   A Latin word, exitus; in French egout, a drain. Sousa derives it from Senn.

Salamandra   سمندر   A lizard.
Samandr.

Sambuco   سبوق سوبق   Boat, or pinnace.

Samerça   سبيسه   An exposed situation, open to the sun.

Sanco   ساق   A bird's leg.
Sak.

Sejana   سجن   Prison. Chain.

Sardam   حرذون   A green lizard from Lybia, the land crocodile.

Sarjento   سرجنك   Sarjeng, a non-commissioned officer; from

		from Ser, head, and Jung, war. In Dutch Serjeant, as in English.
Sarralho	سراي	Saraee, a palace.
Sarraquinos	سراقين	Robbers; from Saraca, to rob.
Seara de trigo	ساكره	Sahra, corn, just before it is cut.
Sebel	سبل	Sebel, vea sebel with two eyes, which physicians call dilatative, or branching. Avicen.
Sega	سكه	A plough, harvest time.
Semide	سبيده	Flower of wheat.
Sirage	سيرج	Oil of gergelim, or sesame, Indian corn.
Sisamina Semsaneeat.	سمسانيات	Saõn os ossos miudos das juncturas dos dedos das mãos, e dos pés. Avic.

Avic. c. 25. p. 15. Sound of the small bones of the joints of the fingers and toes.

Soda   صدع   Sodá. Pain in the head.

Sorvete   شربة   Sherbet, any drink, in Persian and Arabic.

Sottaō   سطوح   Reservoir.

Sumagre   سماق   Sumack, a tree, or shrub.

T.

Tabarzet   طبرزذ   Tabarzad, white sugar-candy.

Tabaxir   طباشير   Sugar of the bamboo.

Tabaz Dabaá Dibo.   ضبع   Tabaz means a leôa, a lioness, and not o lobo, a wolf; and is called Dibo, and not Tabaz.

Tabefe

Tabefe	طبيخ	Tabiche, warm ewe's milk thickened with flour and sugar.
Tabique	طبيق	A division made by boards and hoops, or wattles.
Tufam	توفان	Typhon, a whirlwind.

X.

Xergao	شرك	Hangings.
Xaroco	شروق	An easterly wind, land or sea breeze.
Xaropo	شراب	Syrup. Sherabati, a maker of syrup, a weak wine. Bee keefa, without intoxication.
Xeque	شيخ	Title of honour and dignity.

Xarife

Xarife   شريف   Title of prince in Barbary.

Xauter   شاطر   An experienced guide in the deserts of Arabia.

Xelma   سلما   Snare for birds, or arma-dilha.

Xo   شوْ   A word used in stopping beasts of burden.

Xorcas   شركه   Bracelets and rings that the women wear round the ankles.

Z.

ZABRA   زبره   An African boat.

Zara   زهر   Zehr, a flower. Zehra benet Jesu, a flower of the race of the Messiah, the name of a woman.

Zorame

Zorame	سلهام	Solhame, a white cloak made of the fineſt wool.
Zorzal	زرزور	Zarzur, a ſtarling.
Zerbo	زرب	Zerbon, a term in anatomy, a canal, or duct.
Zigue zigue	زيغ زيغ	The creaking ſound of a door, opening and ſhutting, of a new mat.
Zizania	زوان	Tares, darnel.

APPENDIX.

Kazim-i-buzurg كاظم بزرگ Kazhun, a large branch of a canal; az dur

Xijm xijm زج زج The cracking of a bone, ripe and flaring new fruit.

Zazana زازن Lace, darn

APPENDIX.

THE extract which I have here given, is from Mr. Wilkins's Sanscrita Grammar, and, I may add, Dictionary, which for elegance of type, excellence of arrangement, and lucid order, is far above my praise. The Hitopadesa, or Amicable Instruction, first known by the unmeaning appellation of Pilpay, Elephant's Foot, and Bidpay, Fat, or Splay Foot, Fables, is the original of Æsop, whose real name was Eswed, or Esud, from the Arabic word اسود black. This strengthens the opinion of the Arabs, that Æsop was a Nubian, or Abyssinian; and makes it more than probable, that he and Lokman were one and the same. The knowledge of the primitive language to those who are sent to India, must be of incalculable utility for the discovery of the καιρὸς εὐδαίμων, or lucky moment in the Hindoo Almanacks, which is there pointed out in Sanscrit, and intelligible only to the initiated,

tiated. Thanks to Mr. Wilkins and the accomplished Pundit in the Edinburgh Review, we may now know which day is marked with chalk, and which with coal, in spite of the Brahmans, in whose skulls all the light has been hitherto locked up, as it was heretofore in the lanthorn of Aristotle.

The Sanscrit, Greek, Roman, and German languages, touch in many points, and in nothing more than in their privatives. Soor, good; Asoor, not good; Sutty, faithful; Asutty, unfaithful. Κακὸν, evil; ἄκακον, good. Felix, infelix; and in German, Tugend, virtue; Untugend, vice.

The fables of Bidpai, or Sanscrit Apologues, have, it is well known, undergone a variety of versions into Persic, Arabic, Hebrew, Greek, and Latin, besides Italian, Spanish, and German. The Hebrew, by Rabbi Joel, had disappeared in 1697, when Sebastian Gottofred Starkey, published the Greek and Latin at Berlin; the ancient Latin is directly from the Hebrew, by John de Capua, and the Spanish from the old Latin.

Latin. From the Latin came the German with this title, Beyſpiel der alten Weyſen von Geſchlecht zu Geſchlecht, with one hundred and twenty-five plates. This edition of 1483 is, perhaps, ſtill in the library at Ulm. The Greek verſion was made by Simeon Seth, a phyſician, and by order of Alexis Comnenus, in the eleventh century, and tranſlated by Poſſinus, and ſtill cloſer by Starkius.

My principal intention is to ſhow, that if the metre, which we call hexameter from the number of its feet, is common to four languages, and if the Sanſcrita be proved to be the original, the Greeks, Romans, and Germans have either borrowed it, or fallen into it from ſome unaccountable reſemblance in their language to that of the Hindoos. I may alſo add, that the identity of metre of any four languages, three of which are ancient and one modern, affords no ſmall probability of their dependence and derivation one from the other, eſpecially if that metre conſiſt of dactyls and ſpondees, which are under no obligation for their harmony to the rhythm of blank verſe, or the rhyme of heroick meaſure.

The

The reduction in the Greek, Latin, and German languages, of the cases of nouns, which are more in number in the Sanscrit, and the abridgment of declensions are, no doubt, as strong a presumption of secondary improvement, as that the best dictionary is the last.

The Sanscrit language resembles the Greek and Latin, in the formation of the cases of its nouns, and declensions of its verbs, and particularly in the termination in mi, which it seems, is anomalous in the Greek. I do not know, if this be worth mentioning, as the Sanscrit termination is owing to the pronoun suffixed, as in Asmi, am I; Jivami, live I: but in the Greek there is no trace of the pronoun ἐγώ; none indeed of ἐγώ, but some of Ιω, which was the old Doric mode of writing, as we learn from the Scholiast of Aristophanes, γράφεται καὶ ἰὼ ἀντὶ τοῦ ἐγώ, IΩ is also written for ego, and by dropping the last vowel in δίδωμίω it will be δίδωμι, give I, like the Sanscrit. The word Barbara, a barbarian, claimed by so many languages, and explained by so many etymologists, is Sanscrit; as

is

is also Moorhatā, foolishness, with the Greeks, μωρότης, which they, as they are wont, derived from τὸ μὴ ὁρᾶν in their own language, from not seeing, or from μὴ ὦρα not having foresight.

Maha nandi, in the Bisnagur language, which is Sanscrit, means great pleasure, as it does in Greek; μέγα ἀνδάνειν, to please greatly. Eustathius is reduced to an absurdity in his derivation of μέγα from μὴ γῆ, no longer on earth, but above it.

As it is my design to exhibit a specimen of Greek and Sanscrit parallels at the end of the work, I shall proceed to the main business, and transcribe the Sanscrit verses, placing at their head the name of a priest in Ceylon, whose name is an hexameter.

VELLIVERIEY Sangarakeeta teron wahansey.

1. Ajaramavarat prajno vidyam arthancha chintayet.
2. Grihit'(a) iva Keseshu mrityuna dharman acharet

3. Vidya

(176)

3. Vidya dadati vinayam vinayad yati patratam
4. Patratwad d'hanam aptoti d'hanad dharmas tatah fuckam.
5. Sarva drayeshu vidyaiva vittam ahur anuttaman
6. Aharyatwad anarghyatwat akfhayatwach cha farvada.
7. Sangam nayati viduaiva nichagapi naram farit
8. Samudramiva durdhardfham nripam bhagyamatah param.

THE ENGLISH IN THE ORDER OF THE WORDS.

LIKE one not fubject to ficknefs, and death, a wife man fcience and wealth fhould confider.

N. B. *Cha* at the end of *arthan* means *and*, as the Latin *que* does, and is always joined to another word in both languages.

2. Seized as one by the hairs of the head by death, the duties of religion he fhould practife.

3. Knowledge

3. Knowledge giveth humility, from humility he attaineth worth.

4. From worth, wealth he attaineth, from wealth the power of being religious, from thence happineſs.

5. Of all things knowledge, alſo treaſure is eſteemed the greateſt.

6. From incapacity to be ſtolen, from incapacity to be given away, from incapacity to be deſtroyed.

7. Conducteth knowledge alſo to acquaintance, a man, as

8. The humble ſtream to the ocean, hard to be attained to the prince, to good fortune after this.

GERMAN.

Ein Weiſer ſoll Kentniſs und auch Gluckſguter betrachten,

1. Als der, der kein Sklave der Krankheit, und Sterblickheit iſt.

2. Er ſollte Religion, und deren Pflichte ſo üben Als der, der vom Tode in die Haare ergriffet.

N   3. Kentniſs

3. Kentniſs ſchenket Demuth, Demuth Krönt ihm mit Würde.
4. Durch Würde Komt Reichthum, und Gewalt giebt um ſelig zu ſeyn.
5. Sey Kentniſs dein groſſeſter Schatz, und unmöglich muſs werden
6. Eigene Verſchenkung, Raubung, Zernichtung von Feinden.
7. Sanft ſchleicht ſich der Bach zum Weltmeere, wie Weiſeit zu Freunden,
8. Und Freunde zum ſtolzen Fürſten, die beglucken das Leben.

GREEK.

Δεῖ σοφον ἄνδρ' ἄθρειν, Θεὸς ὡς, γνῶσίν τε κ̀
ὄλβον·
Ζῆνα σέβειν ὡς ἔν τις θριξὶ μόρῳ ἐπίληπτος·
Γνῶσις ἔδωκε τάπεινα, κ̀ ἄξιον ἔμμεναι ὄλβου·
Ἐξ πλούτου θρήσκοντι θεῶν ἔξεσῖι γένεσθαι,
Καὶ μακάρῳ· πάντων δὲ δαημοσύνη μὲν ἀρίστη.
Ἣν οὐδεὶς κλέπτειν, δύναται, δωρεῖν, ἢ ἀμερδειν.
Εἰς ἄνδρας δὴ Γνῶσις ἄγει, ὡς εἰς ἅλα πήγη,
Εἰς βασιλῆα δυσάμβατον, εἰς εὐδαίμονα καιρόν.

LATIN.

LATIN.

VIR sapiens, tanquam Deus, alta mente reponat
Doctrinamque et opes, et sicut morte prehensus
Summo in crine caput, colat alti numina cœli.
Scire humilem facit; atque humili non dignior
   audit
Divitiis; opibusque datur divina potestas
Numina adorandi, ante obitum dicique beatus.
Optima doctrina est ante omnia, quàm neque
   furta,
Quam neque dona valent, neque rerum abolere
   vetustas;
Illa hominum ad cætus quoque ducit, ut ad
   mare rivus,
Difficilemque aditu regem, vitamque beatam.

To these Sanscrit hexameters may be added the motto, in two verses of six feet, to Mr. Wilkins's Grammar, and the distich at p. 34.

Sausha Dasaratha Rama, Sausha raja Yudhishth'hira,
Sausha Karna maha Tayaga, Sausha Bhima maha vala.

Ille hic Dasarathi natus Rama, rex Udishth'hira
Ille hic largus opum Karna, et Bhima robore
    magno.

For a specimen of a Sanscrit pentameter we have a description of the seasons, as they succeed one another in Hindostan, in a single line of five feet.

Seesar, heemant, Vasant, Greeshma, Varsa, Surat.
Dewy, cold, mild, hot, rainy, dry, or breaking up of the rains. See notes to the Geeta.

Mahabala, or Maha Vala, is a title of the king of Seenghala Dweepa, who is called in the Hitopadesa, the Sarasa Mahabala. Heetopades, p. 258.

I shall

I shall conclude this Appendix with a few Sanscrit words, out of a considerable number, which are found to have the same meaning in other languages.

Sanscrit.	Greek.	Persian.	English.	French.	Latin.
Eka	—	یک	Each	—	—
Aper	—	—	After	Après	—
Dakshina	—	—	—	—	Dextima. N.B. The ancients said for dextro et sinistro, dextimo et sinistimo, Festus. Sallust. Bell. Jugurth. c. 100.

Pratam

Sanscrit.	Greek.	Persian.	English.	French.	Latin.
Pratam First.	πρᾶτον	—	—	—	—
Charam Last	—	اخر Akir	—	—	—
Mayata He dies	—	ماتا Mata, he is dead, in Arabic.	—	—	—
Datum To give	—	دادن	—	Spanish.	Datum Given
Da	—	دَ	—	—	Da, give
Vara A hero	—	—	—	Varon A man, in Spanish.	Baro a soldier.
Pura Become full	—	پر Pur	—	—	—
Nabha, hurds by seizing for- cibly, un- awares.	—	—	Nabs	—	—
Tapa Shines	—	تابان تابیدن Splendor, to shine.	—	—	—

Mana

Sanscrit.	Greek.	Persian.	English.	French.	Latin.
Mana	—	معني	—	—	—
Know, Mind.		Minding, being anxious about. Arabic.			
Lupa	—	—	Lopped, cut off.	—	—

INDEX

INDEX OF NAMES.

Ambrosio Morales, p. xvii.
Abderrahman, — Introduction, p. v.
Alphons VIIIth, p. xv.
Alhambra, p. xxvi.
Alfaisuli.
Arabian Sappho, p. xvi.
———— tale, p. 122.
———— proverb, p. 136.
Alixares de Granada, p. xxvi. Alixar is a term of builders, a jamb of a door, any thing that covers an edifice, or a body, from ازر azara in the Second Conjugation.
Ben Tafufa (Yahya), p. 114.
Cervantes, — Advertisement.
Calecut, p. 112.
Cafiri, p. xvi.
Correa de Serra, p. xxx.

Diarbekr, p. 115.
Deguignes, p. xiv, xv.
Duarte Nunes de Leao, p. 108.
Ebn Haukal, p. 39.
Fines, p. 116.
Florez, p. xvi.
Gagnier, p. 9.
Haleem, p. 122.
Harras, p. 116.
Hormuz, p. 120.
Heetopades,—Appendix.
Hexameters,—Appendix
Julian, Count, — Introduction, p. i.
King, p. 122.
Letters to and from Don Manoueel, p. 109.
Milton,—Advertisement.
Martel, Charles,—Introduction, p. vi.
Manoueel, p. 109, 112, 115.
————, de Faria, p. 108.

Notice of an Arabic MSS. on Agriculture, in the twelfth Century, p. xxix.
Ormus, in Persian Hormuz, p. 115.
Proverb, Span. p. xix.
Plat, Gerald, p. xxx.
Question of Haleem, p. 122.—Like the Abbé Mauri's, to the Parisians. Would you see better were I on the lantern post?
Roderic,—Introduction, p. 1.
Shakespeare,—Advertisement.
Sybarites, p. xxxvii.
Sousa, John, p. 108.
Scholiast of Aristoph.—Appendix.
Sanscrit,—Appendix.
Turrecremata, p. xxxiv.
Vasco da Gama, p. 110.
—— Fernandes, p. 121.
Usted, Sir, p. 100.
Wife, p. ix.
Wilkins,—Appendix.
Xaquimate, p. 101.
Xeque Xarave, p. 101.
Yahya, p. 114.
Zagri, p. xxxii.
Zeit aben Zeit, p. xxi.

ERRATA.

Page.
40. السغت *read* السغاطه
68. houseman, *read* horseman.
155. صجل, *read* صنجل